Aerial Surveys

April 2, 1958

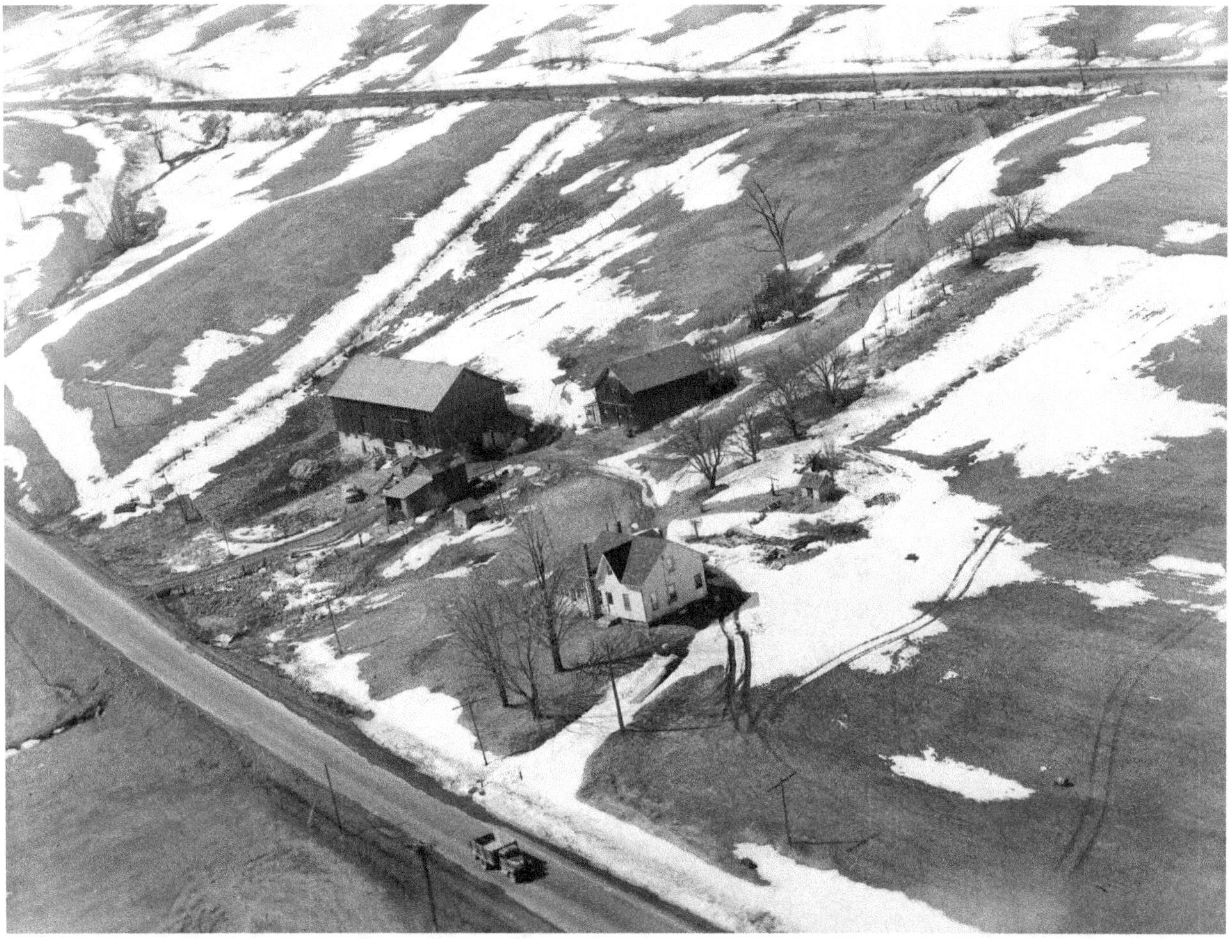

242-237 Vance Smith Farm (formerly Jay & Howard Brown farm), all barns
gone house recently remodeled.

Compiled by J. Roy Dodge and Bill Casey

From the collection owned by Aerial Surveys, Rochester, NY

About these Aerial Photos

Commercial sales of aerial photographs of rural properties started just after World War II with two companies selling their photos to New York State residents. These companies were the Mason Brother's Flying Service from Geneva, NY and Aerial Surveys of Rochester, NY. Mason Brother's went out of business in the mid 1950's while Aerial Surveys maintains their complete collection of negatives and still provides a printing service.

The main method of selling aerial photographs was with the use of a door-to-door sales person. The sales person would show the printed photograph to the property owner hoping that the speculative venture by the photographer would result in a sale. If the owner was not interested in making a purchase at the time the photo was shown, they would forfeit any further opportunity to view or purchase the photo. The authors have searched for the last 8 years without the good fortune of locating the Mason brother's negative collection. But we did locate the collection of Aerial Surveys.

Aerial Surveys owner Joyce M. DeWolf has allowed the reprinting of the following 1958 collection of negatives to allow the general public a second chance to view and perhaps make a purchase. Aerial Surveys can be reached at:

Aerial Surveys   aerialsurveys@rochester.rr.com

PO Box 12554

Rochester, NY 14612

(585) 663-8231

Photo-editing and publishing by Bill & Joanne Casey

Bill5308@aol.com

ISBN: 978-1-329-85039-2

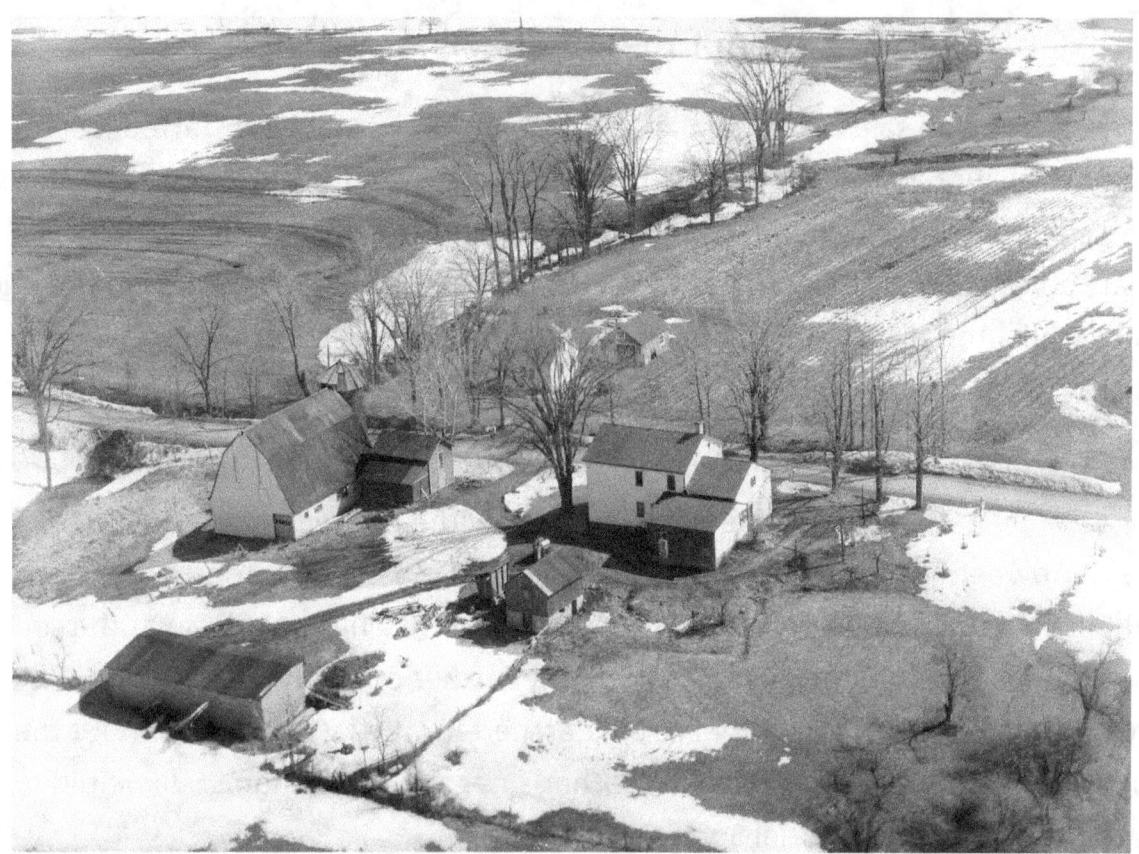

242-191 Frank Williams farm on Webb Road off Route 20. Later became Gernhardt pottery shop. Gernhardt came in 1963 to SU as Professor of Ceramics. Barn and house are still standing.

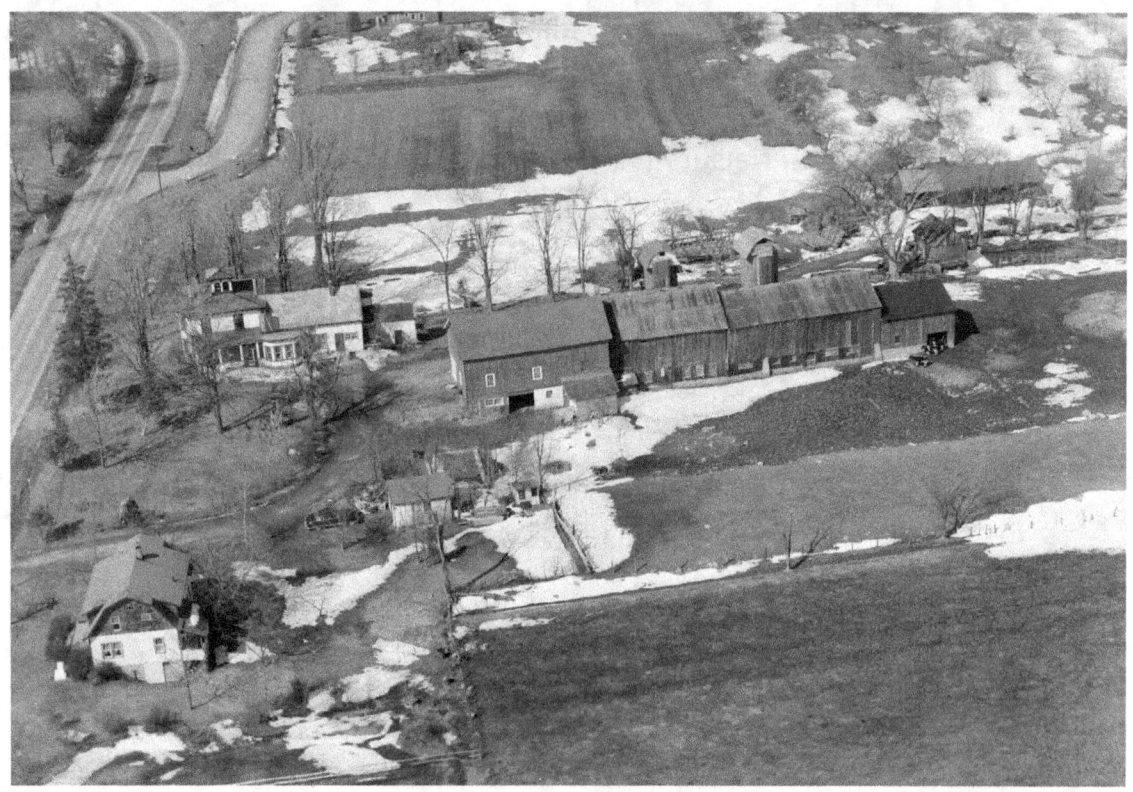

242-192 Laurence Baker farm Route 20 & Webb Rd. All barns burned down in 2010.

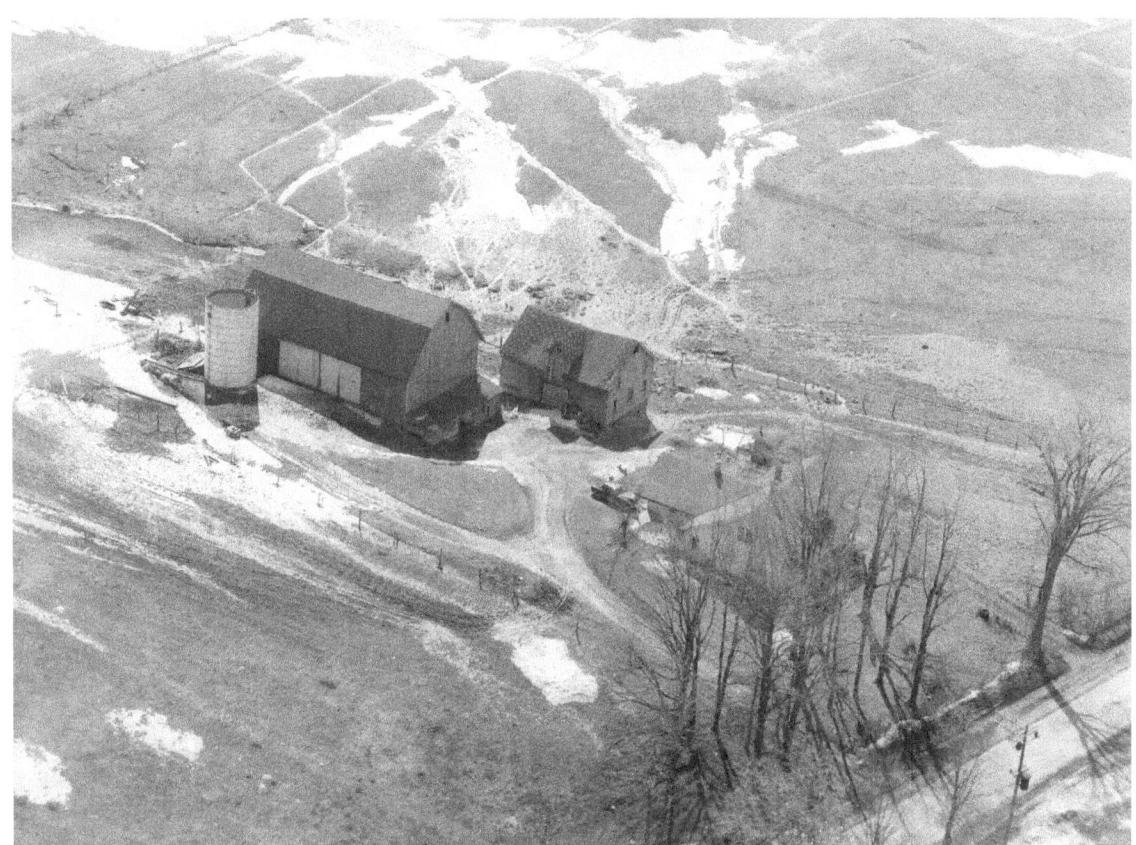

242-193 Owen Carroll farm Route 11. Last raised frame barn (1906) in town of LaFayette. All building burned down in early 1970's.

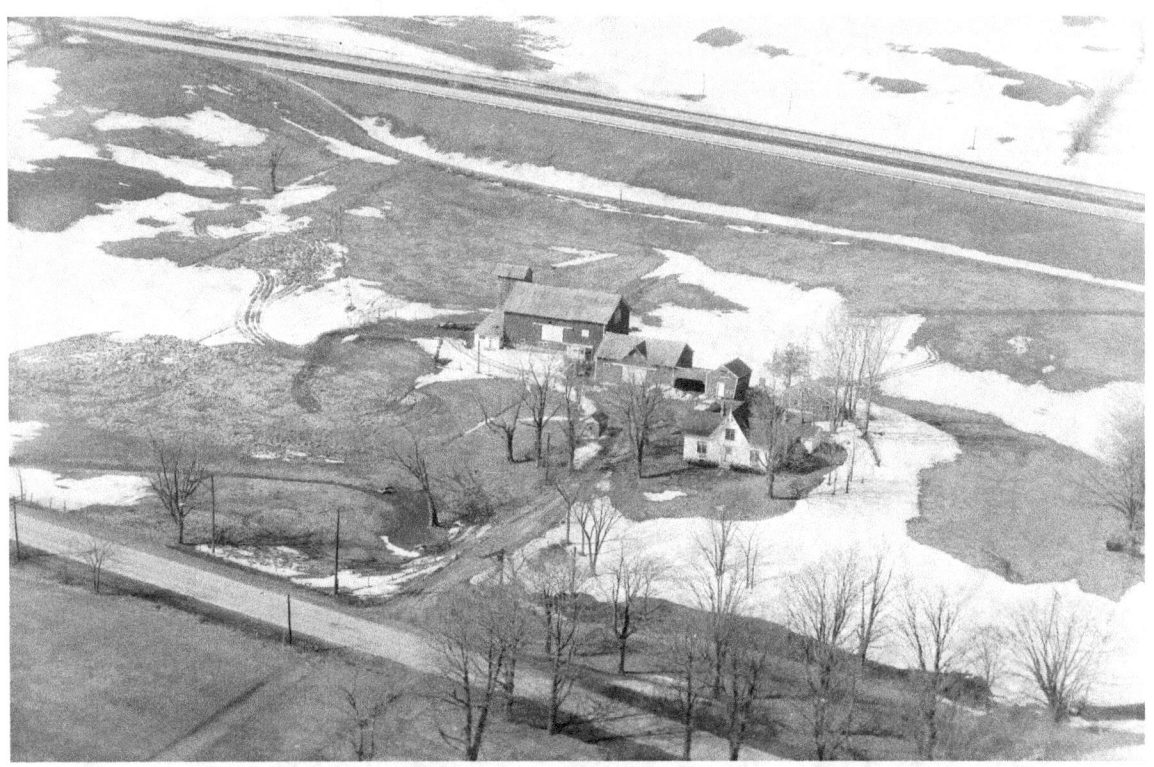

242-194 Robert Mason farm Route 11. All farm buildings gone and house is in ruins.

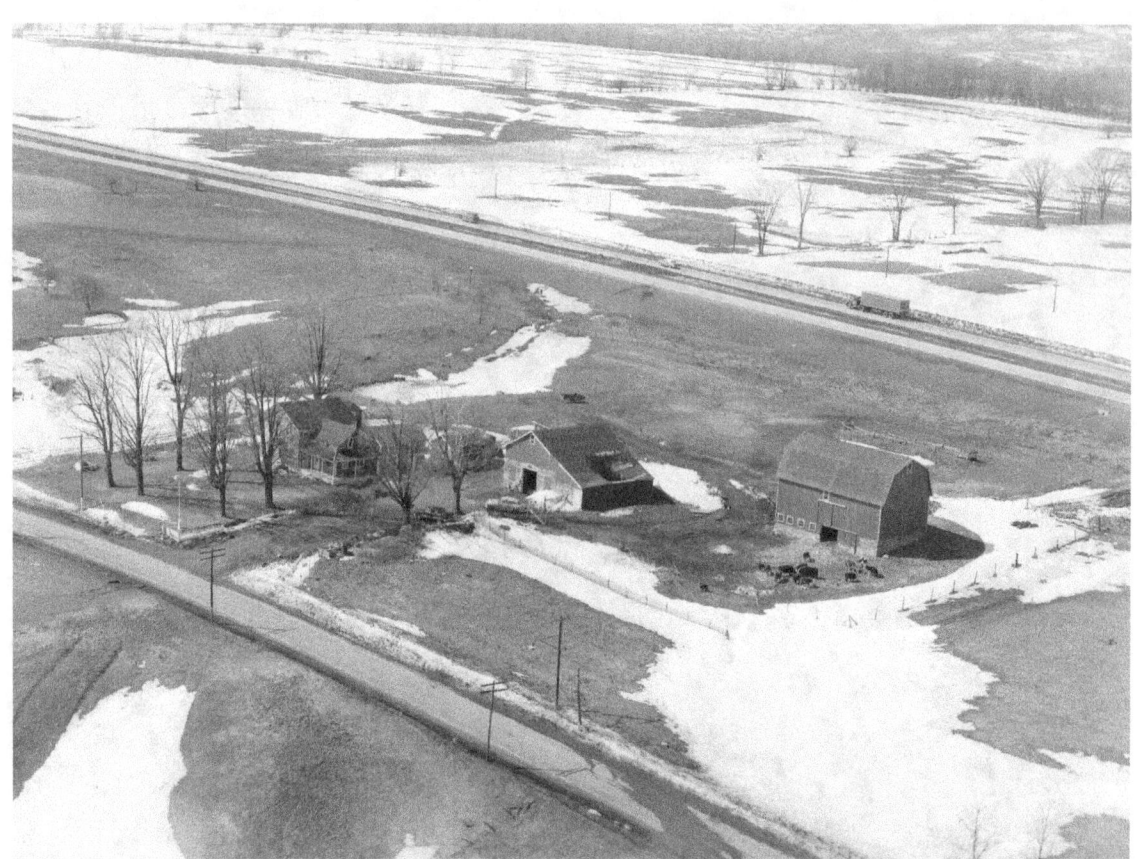

242-195 Frank Amidon farm Route 11. All buildings gone.

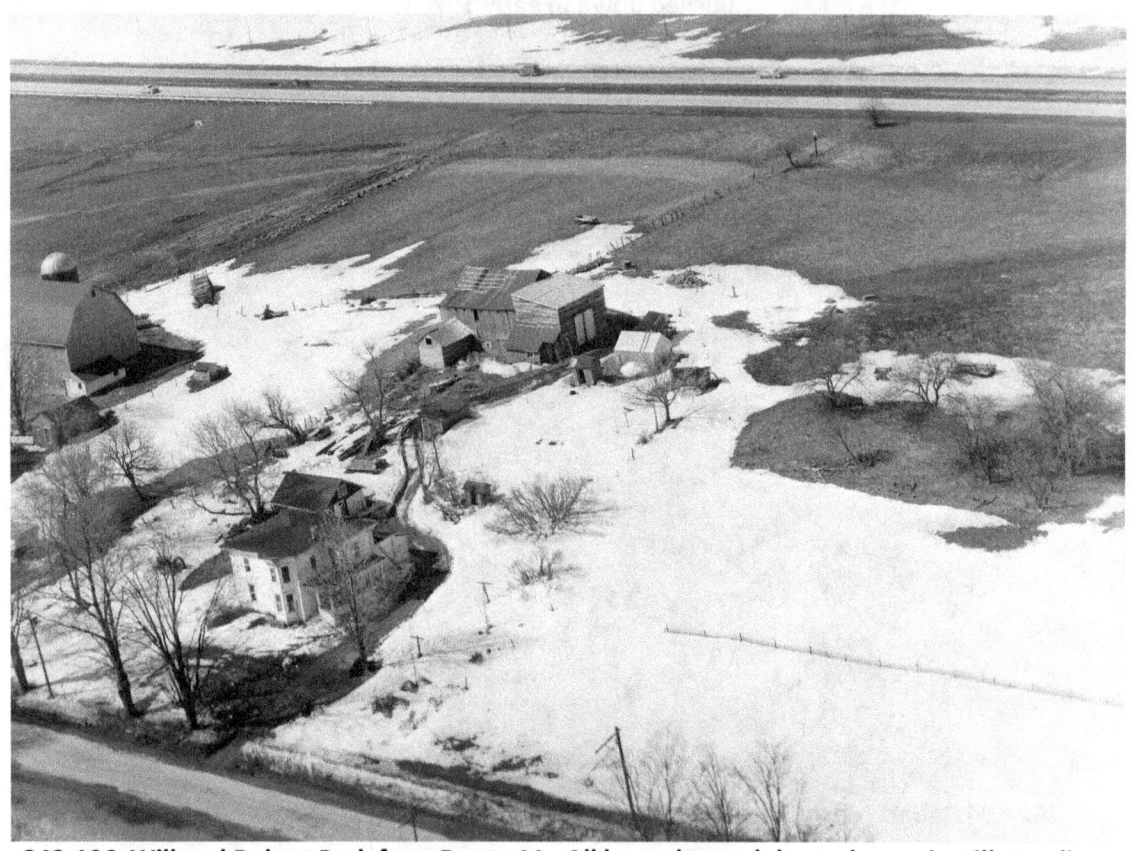

242-196 Will and Robert Park farm Route 11. All barns burned down, house is still standing.

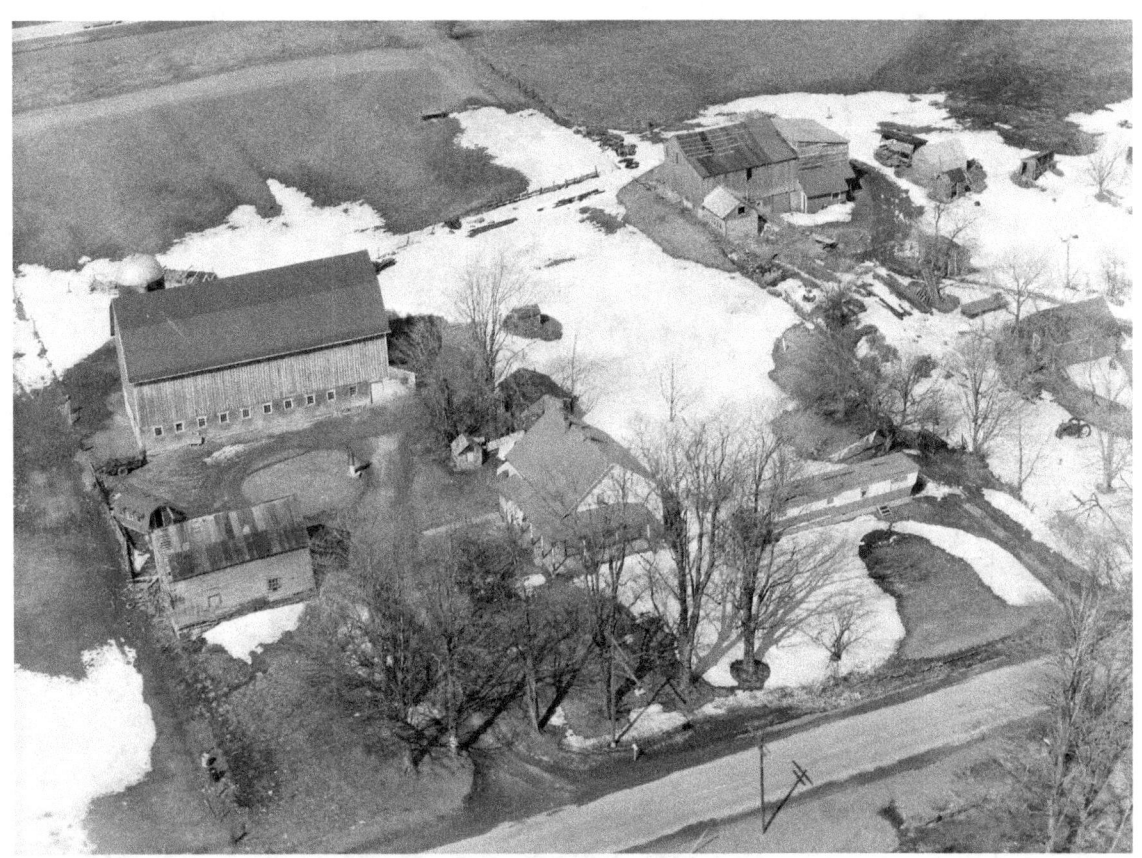

242-197 Henry Carroll farm Route 11. New barn built in 1948. Main barn and house still standing.

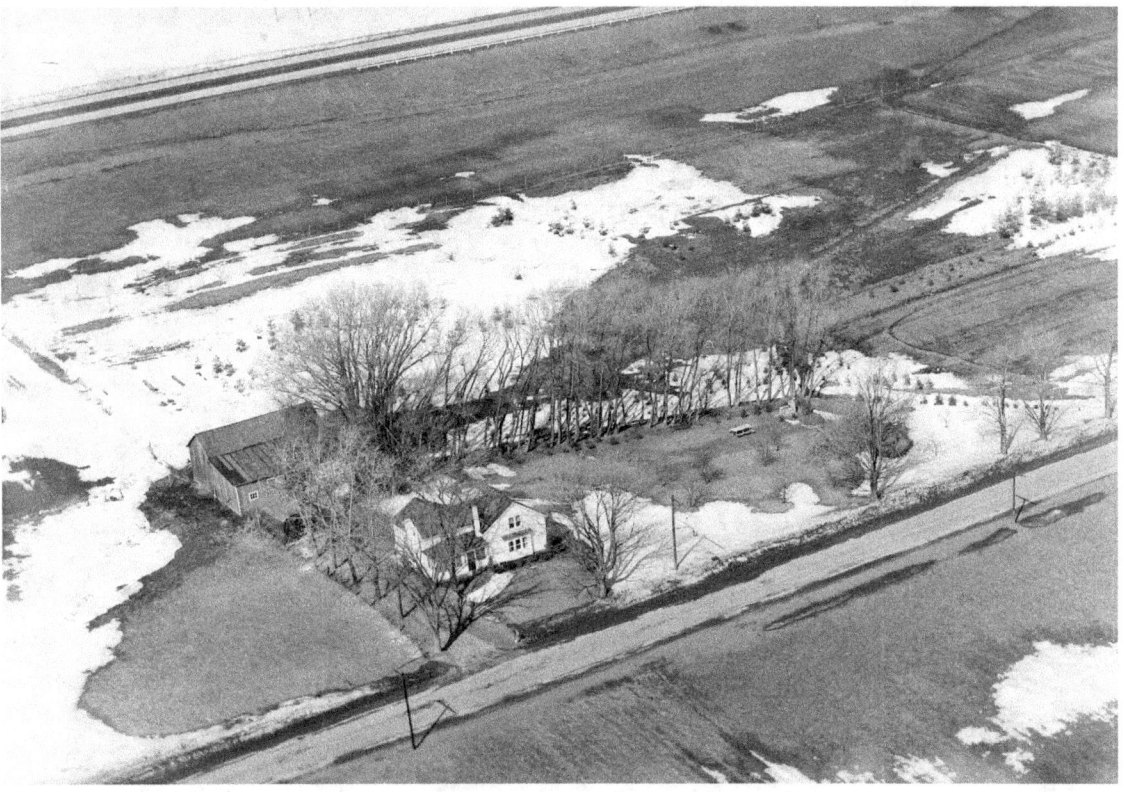

242-198 Byron Brown farm Route 11. The barn is gone while the house is still standing.

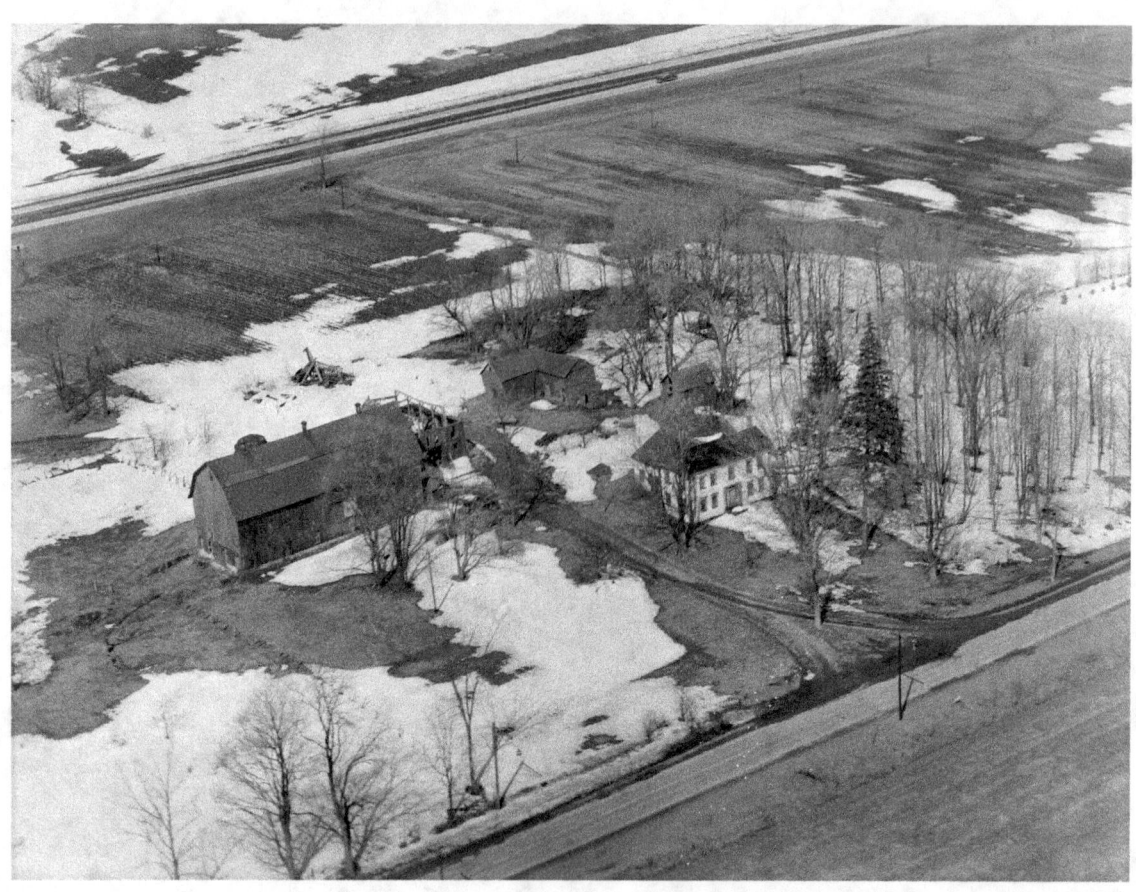

242-199 Edward Dobbins farm Route 11. Barn was fist balloon frame (1911) in LaFayette. All building burned down in the 1970's.

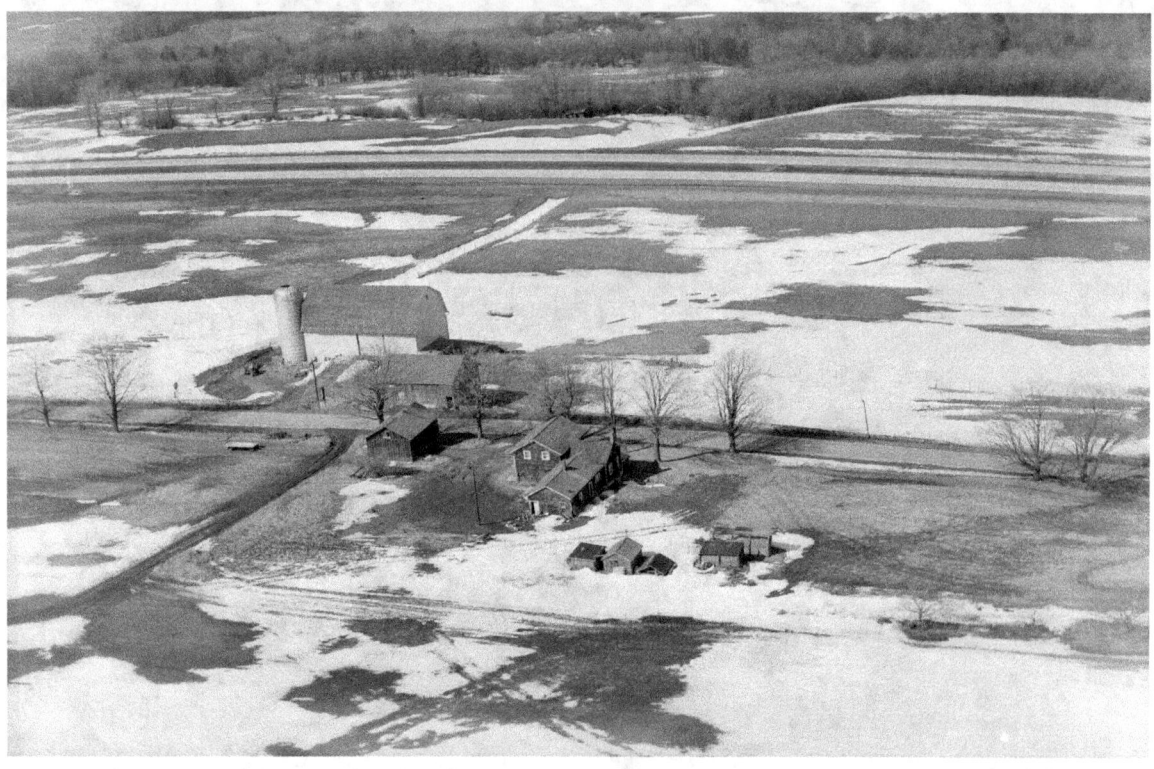

242-200 Gordon Gage farm Route 11. New barn 1936. House and main barn still standing.

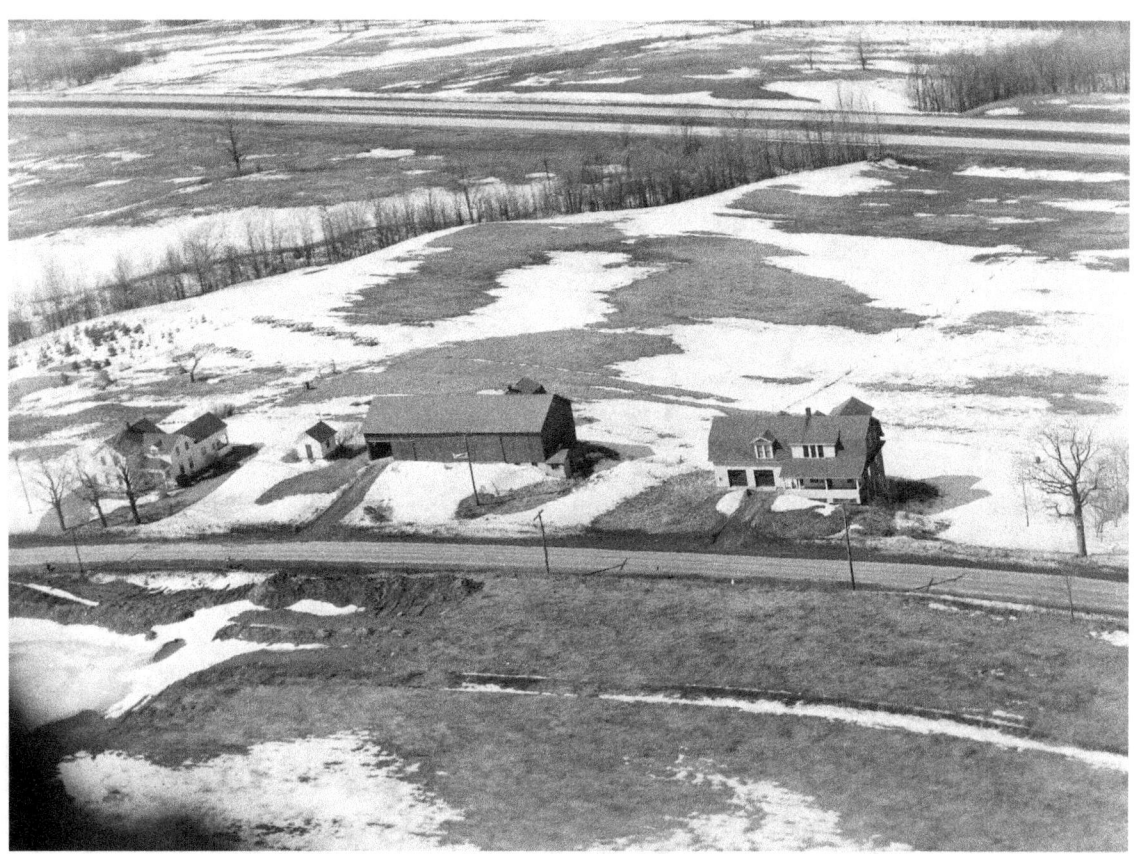

242-201 Charles Barton farm Route 11. Barn torn down.

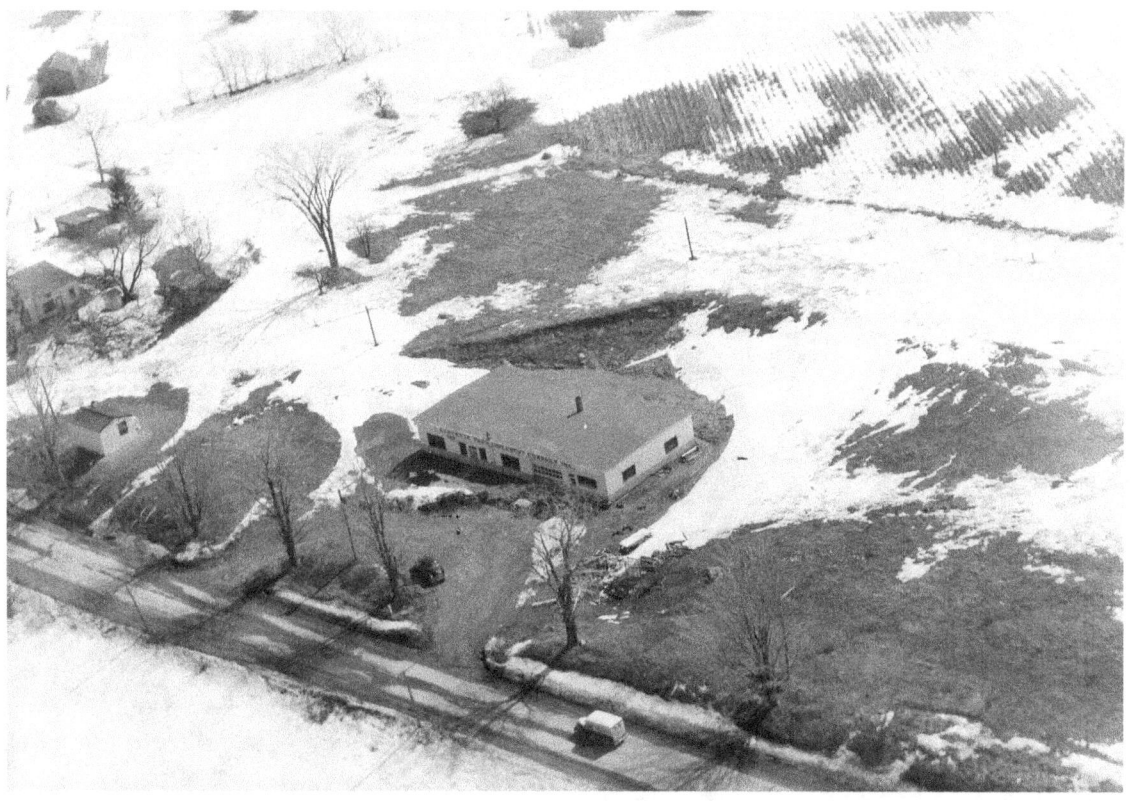

242-202 "LaFayette Farm Machinery Company" Route 11. Now "U-File UM Binding Company".

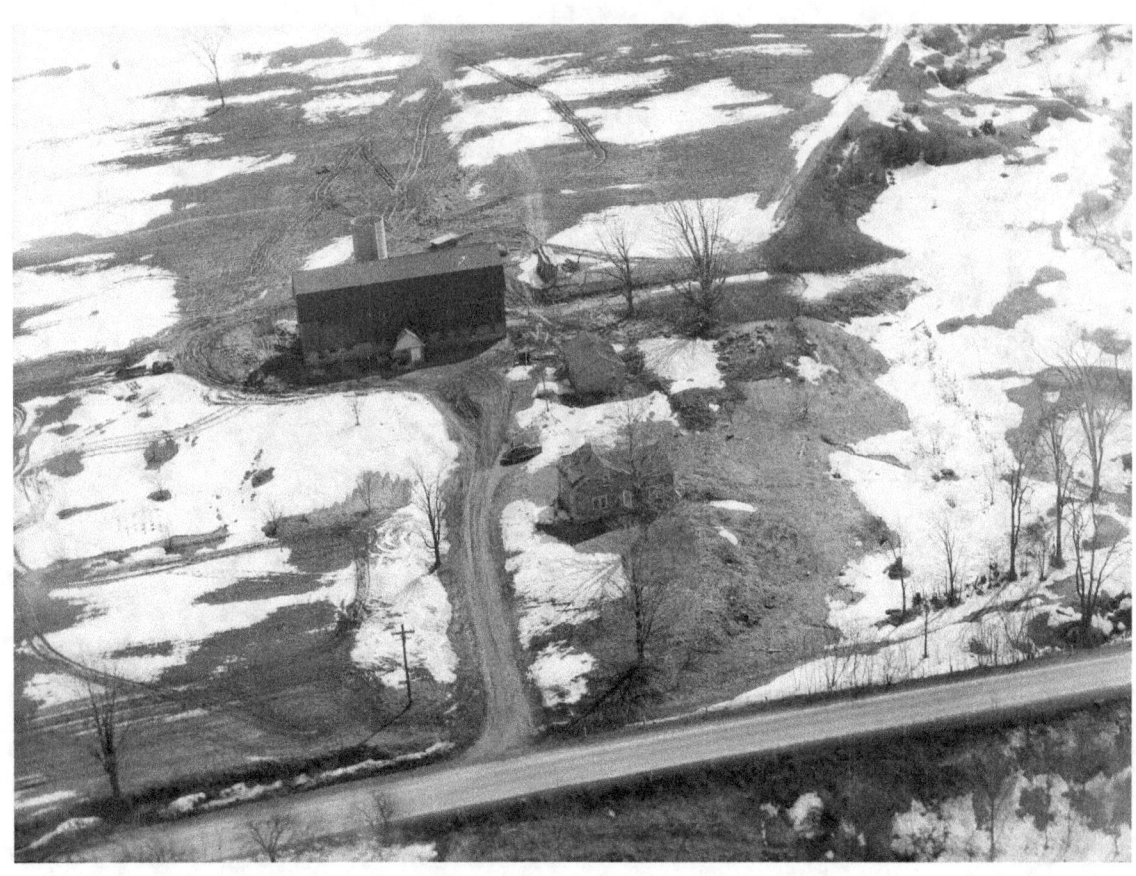

242-203 Thaddeus Ezick farm Route 11 @ North Road. Barn now gone.

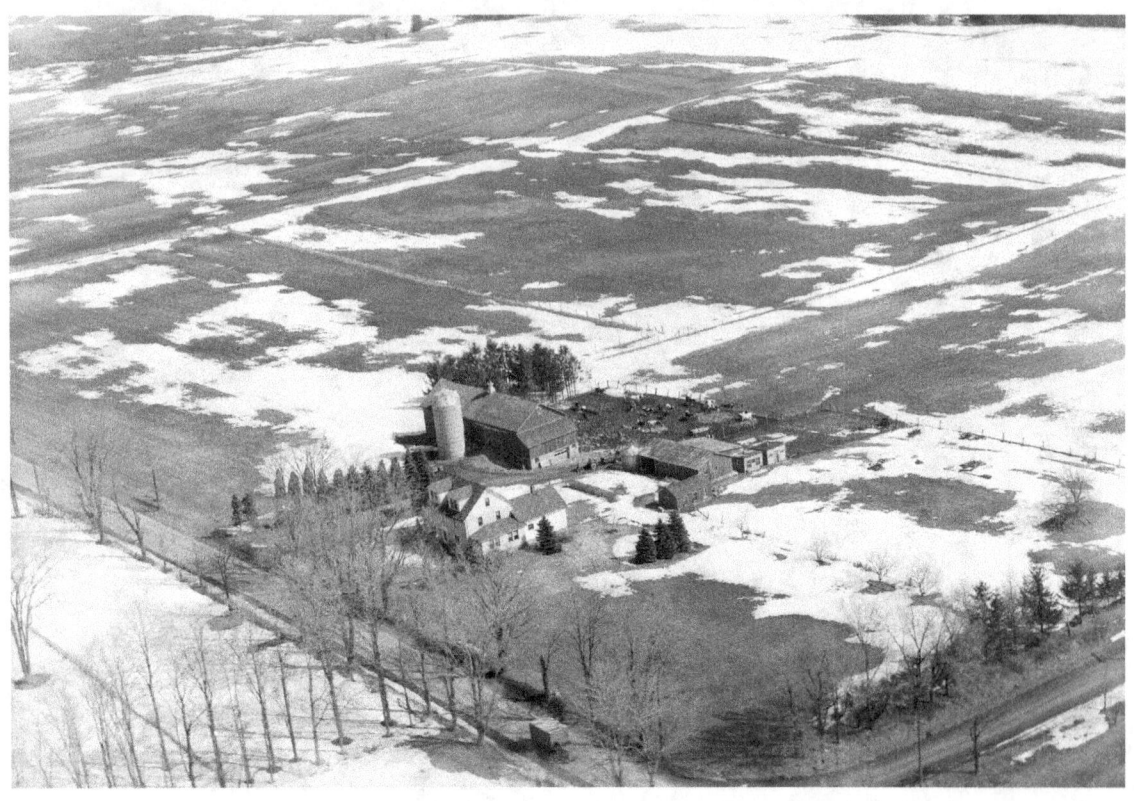

242-204 Bruce Stahl farm Route 11 @ Meeker Road. Barn burned down in the 1970's, house still standing.

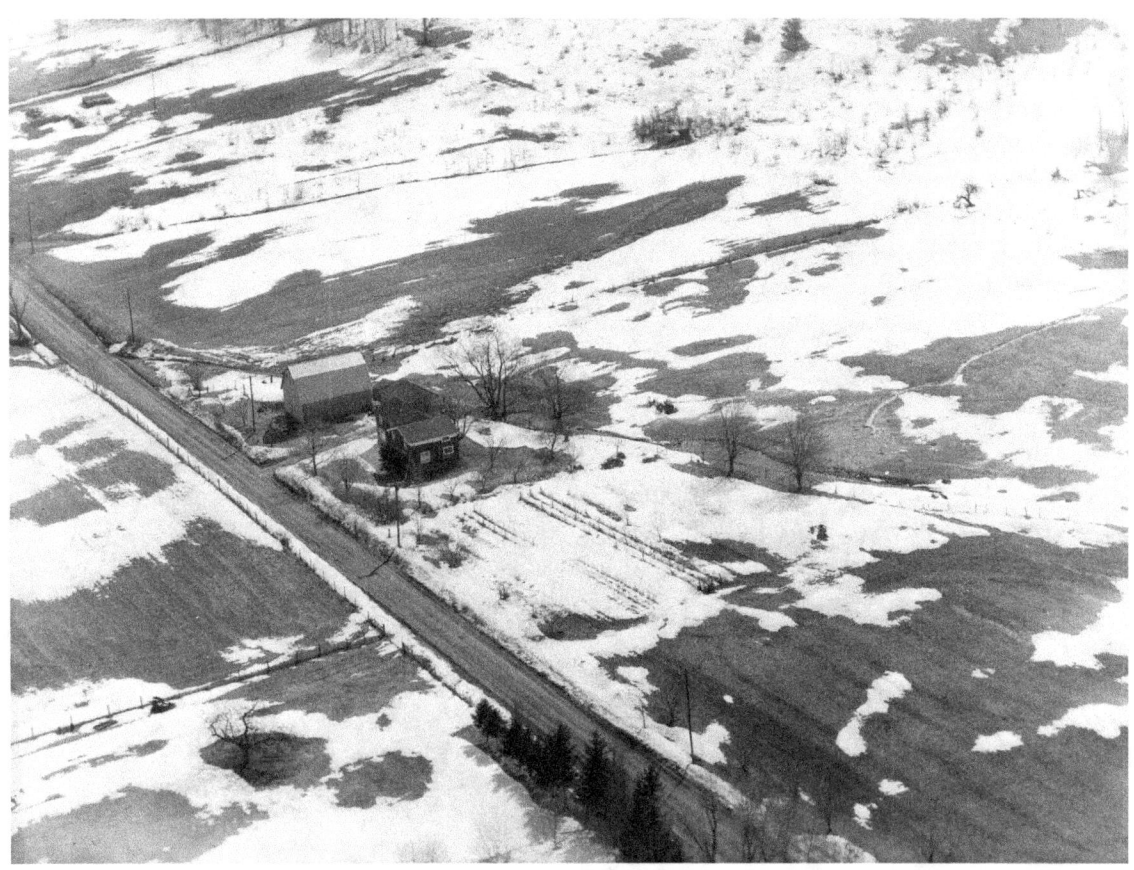

242-205 Murray Russell place Meeker Road @ Route 11. Buildings still standing.

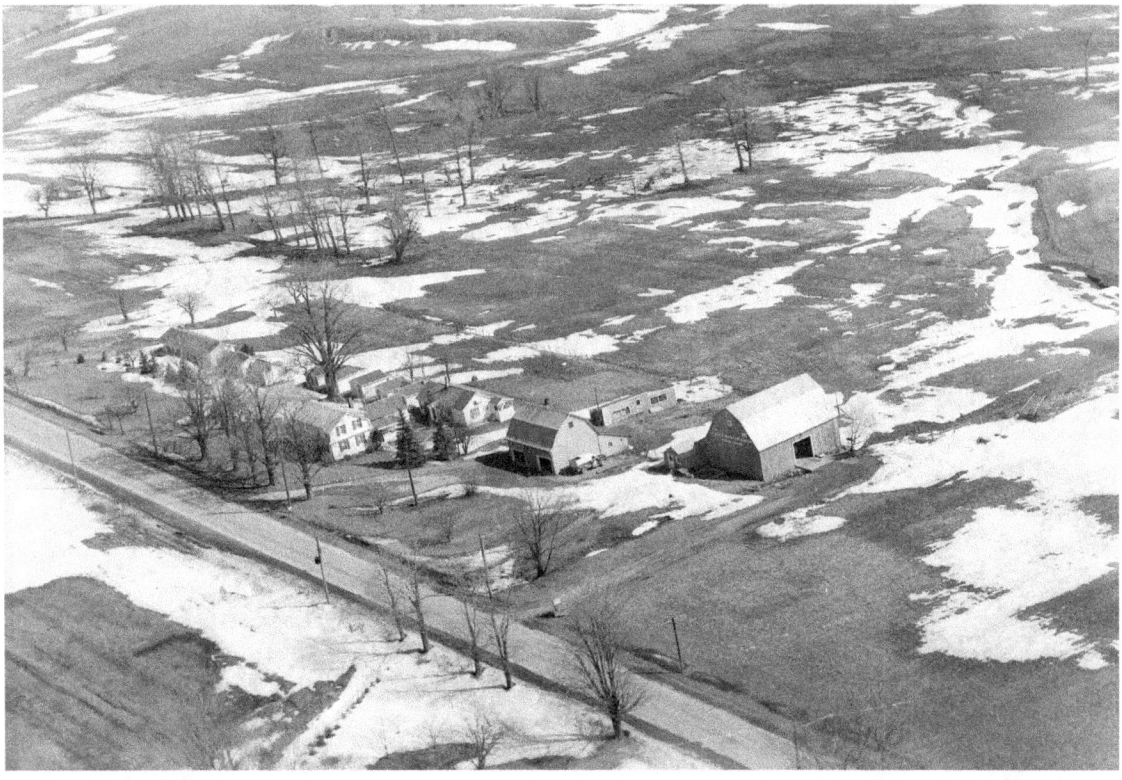

242-206 Study Maple Motel (east side) Route 11. Run by Muriel Riffanacht Whitford.

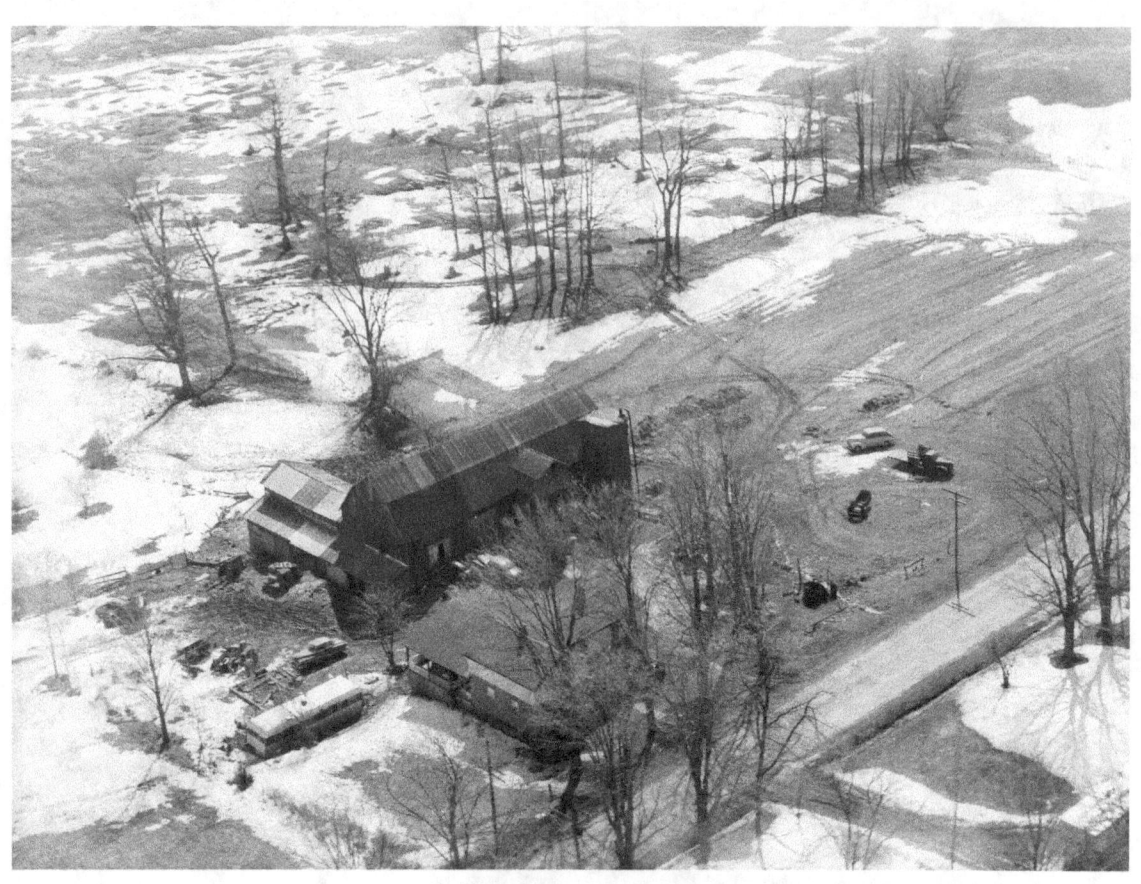

242-207 LeRoy Baker farm east side of Route 11. Barn fell down.

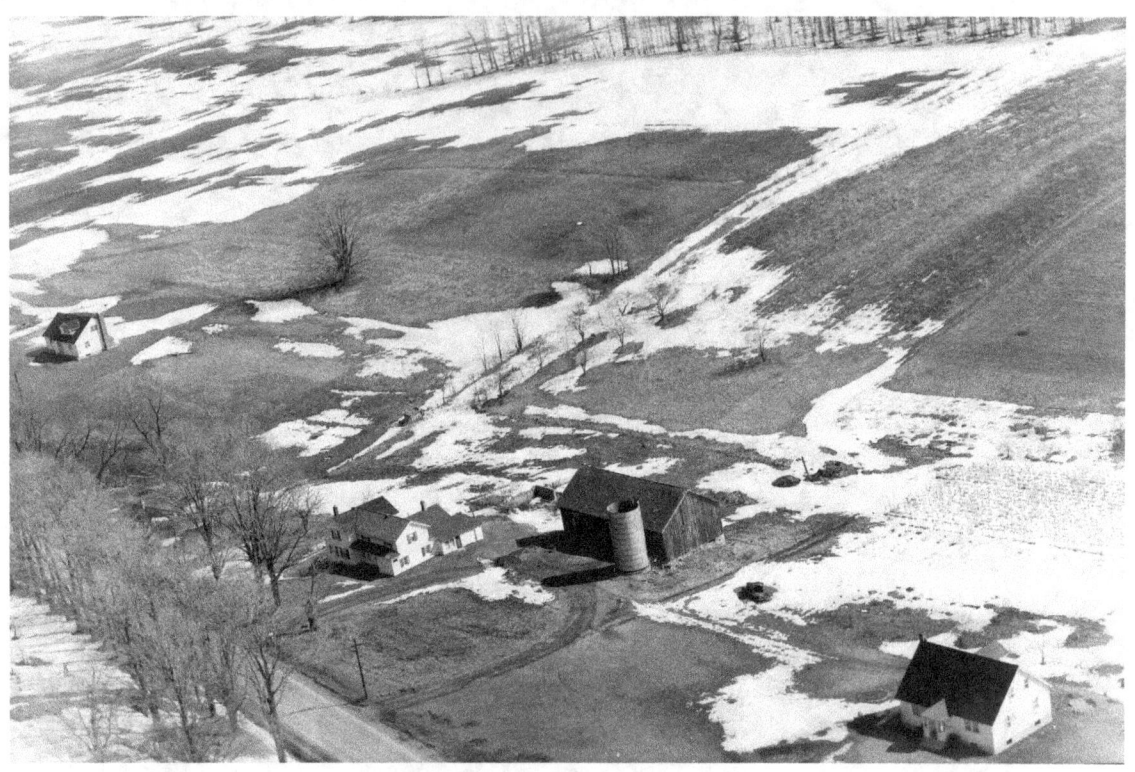

242-208 Alfred Klaiber farm east side of Route 11. Buildings are still standing.

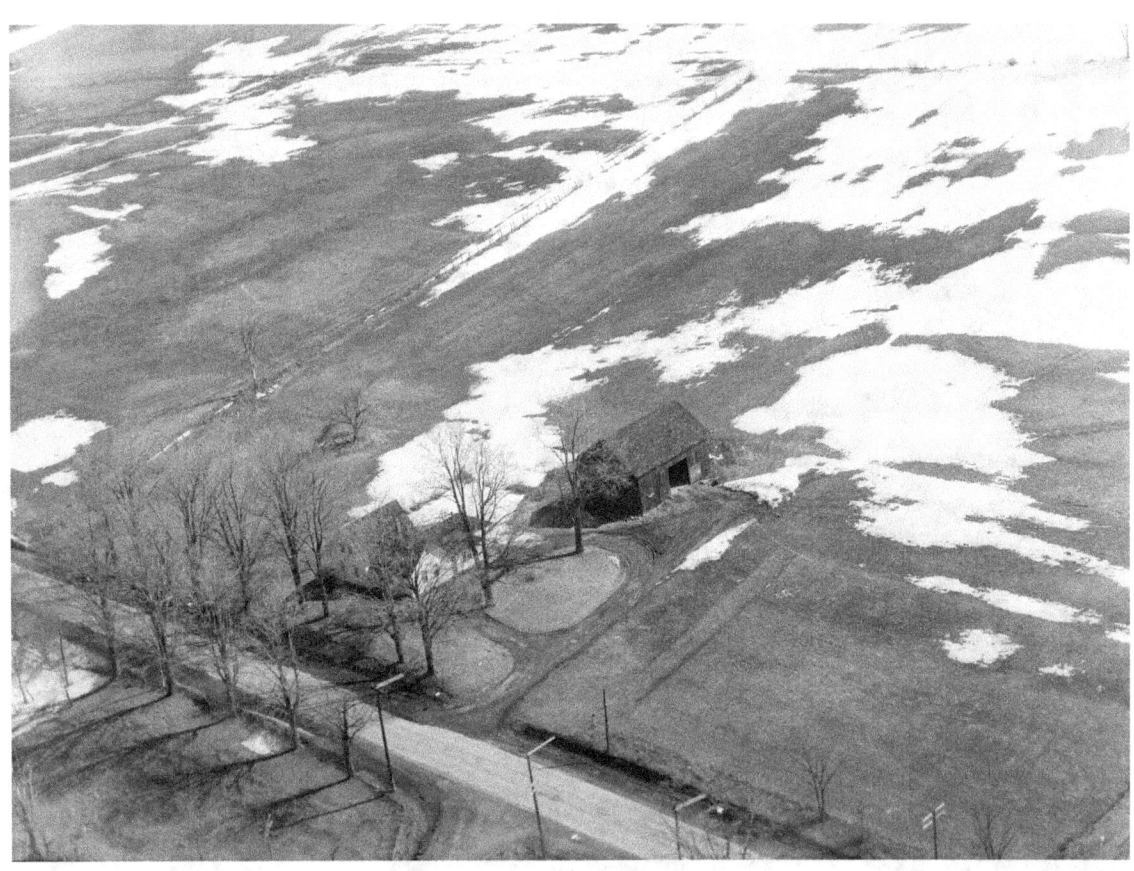

242-209 Fred Stafford place Route 11.

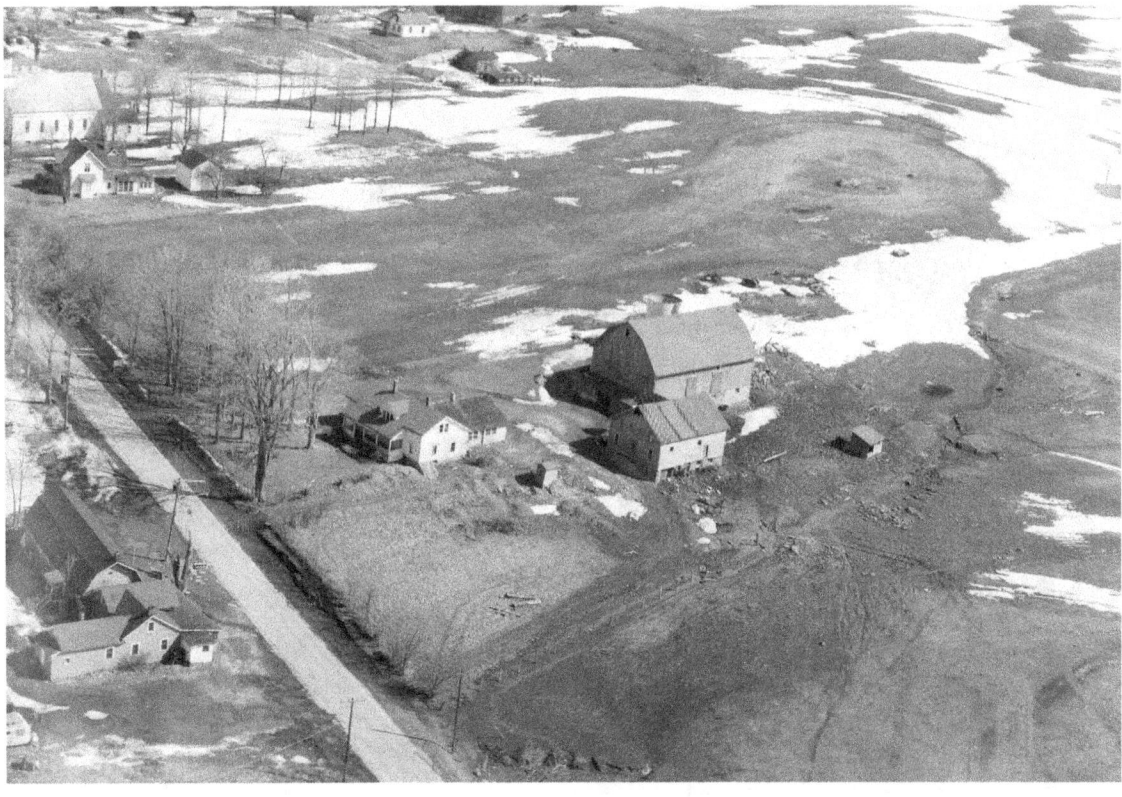

242-210 Owen Carroll farm same as photo 193 but different view. All buildings gone. LaFayette Inn on left.

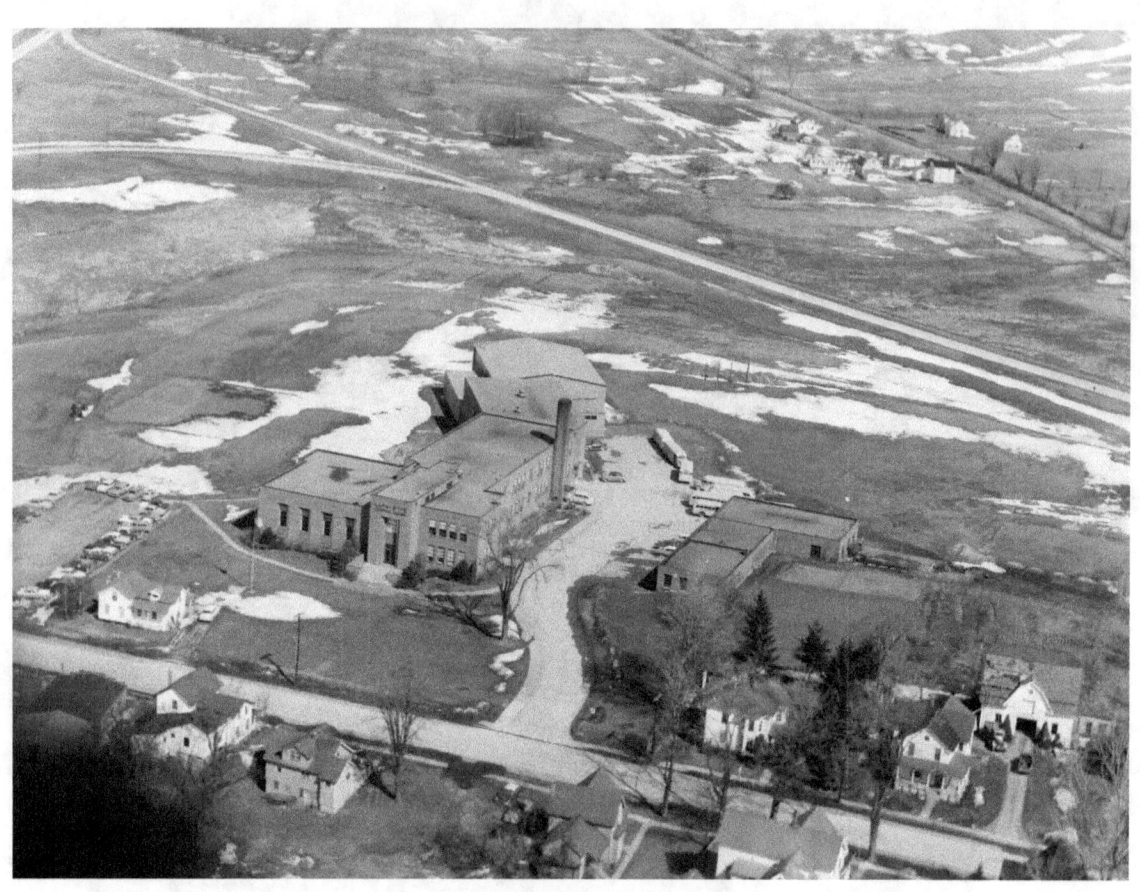

242-211 LaFayette Central School.

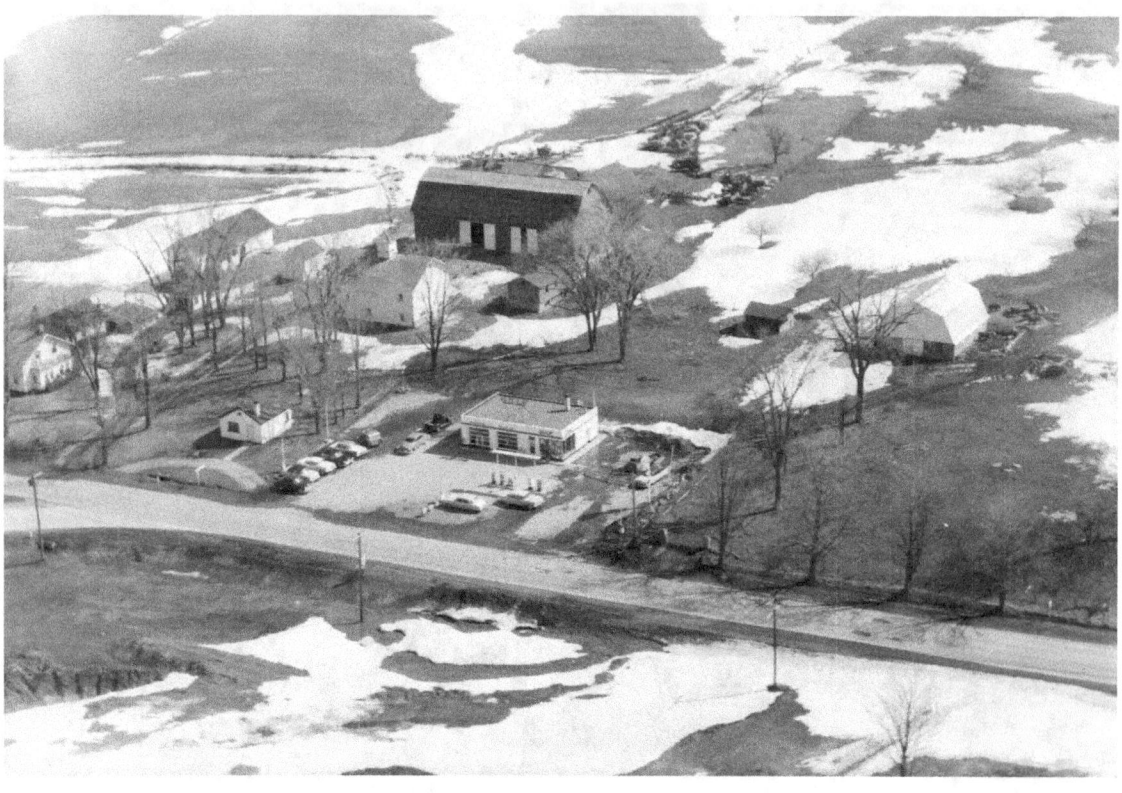

242-212 Gulf gas station built in 1957. Now the site of "Nice & Easy" and Clark farm. Owned in 1958 by Alfred Mallett.

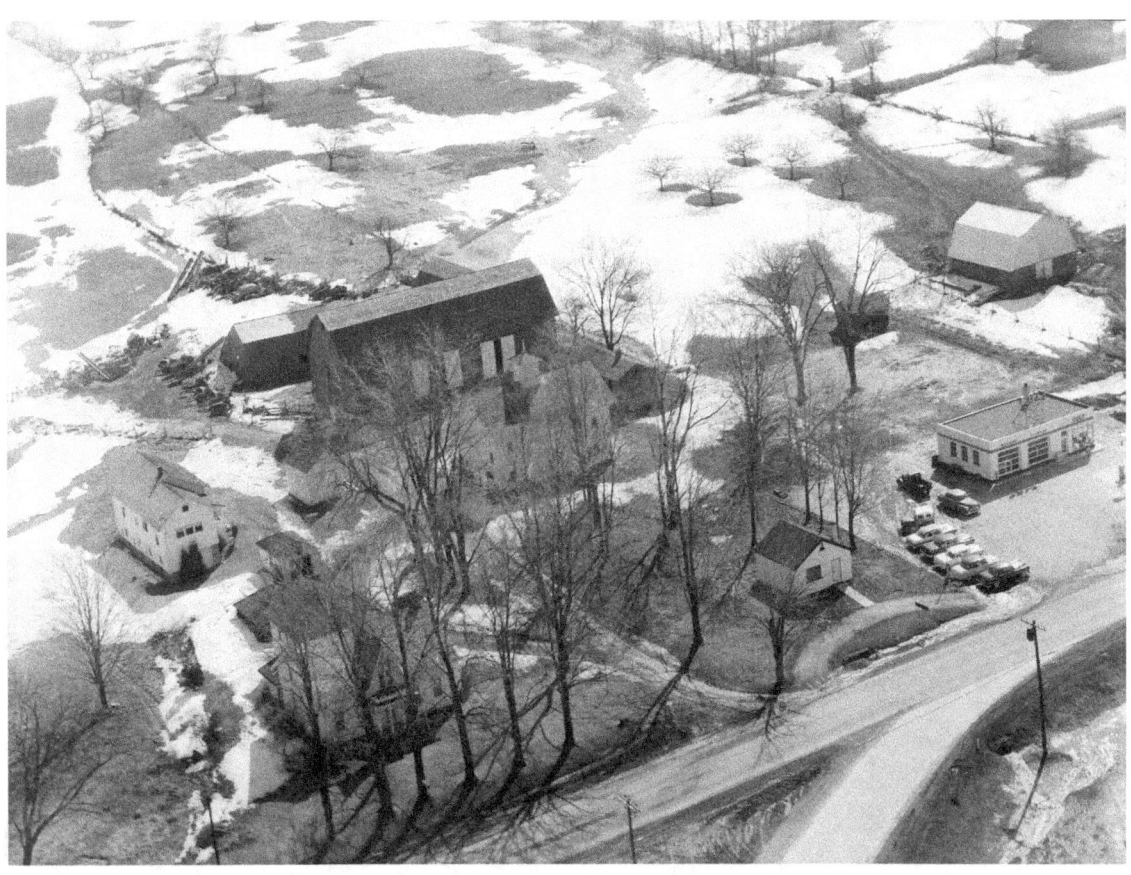

242-213 Clark farm Route 11. All barns burned or torn down. Bell Telephone building in middle, built 1951.

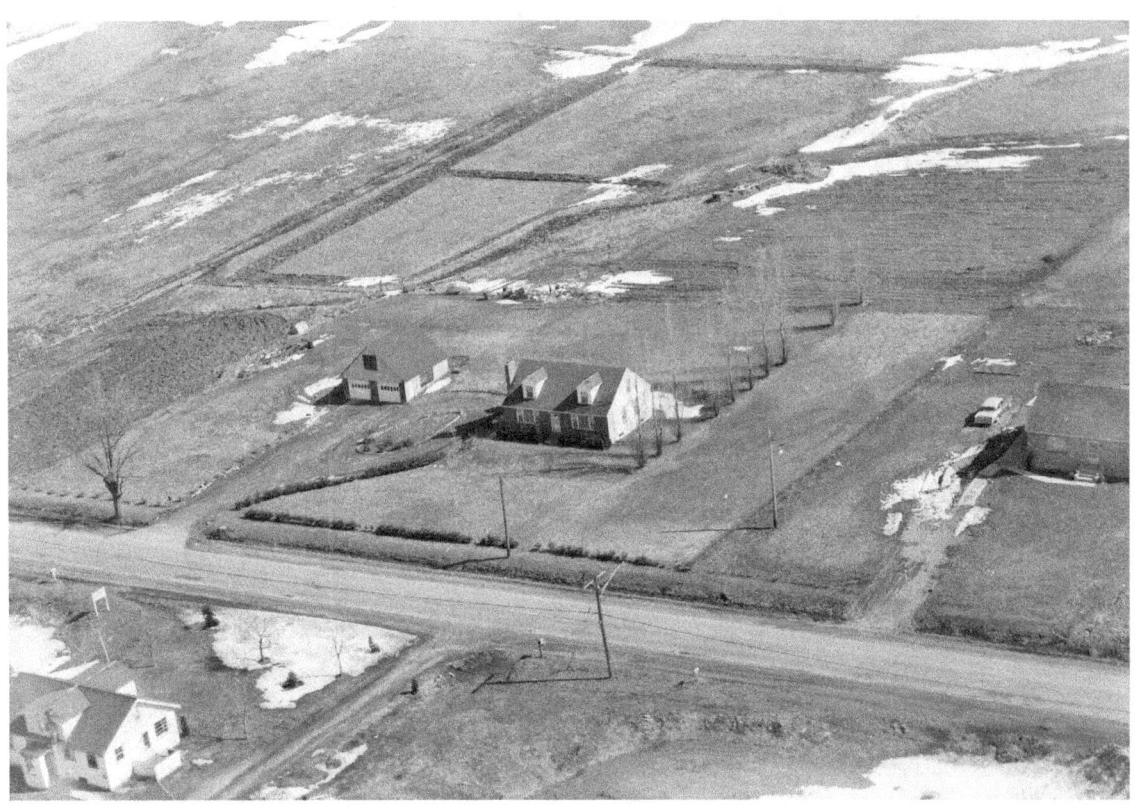

242-214 Galutz house Route 11 built c.1950.

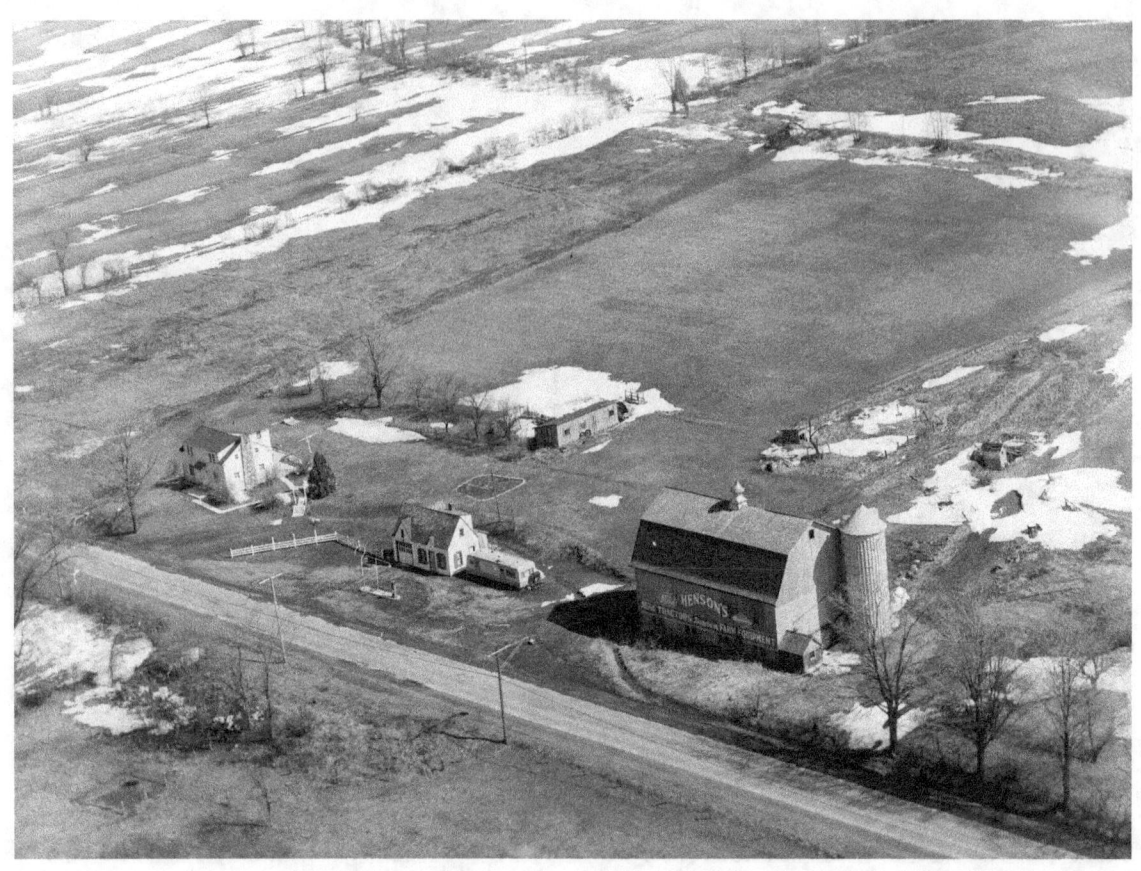

242-215 William Murray farm & Henson's "Ford Tractors & Farm Supply". Gas station built about 1933 now gone. Barn built 1930 and in poor condition.

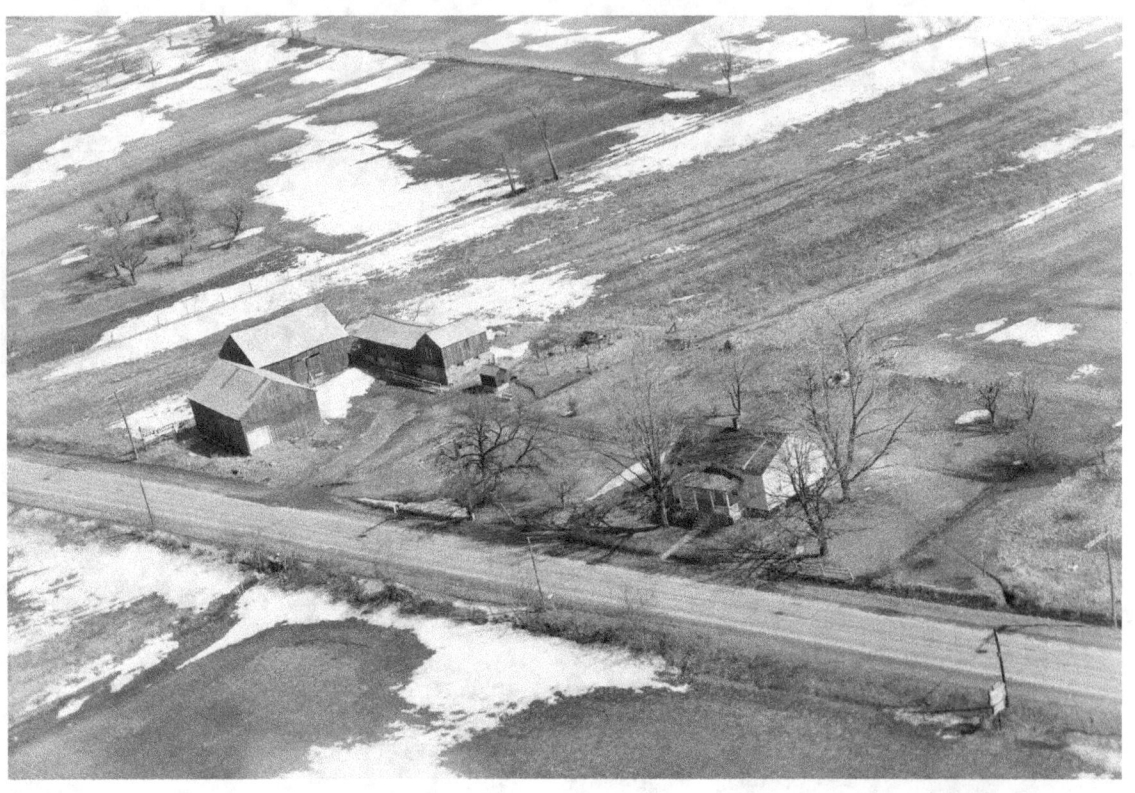

242-216 William Moltion formerly John Long farm Route 11. Barns all gone.

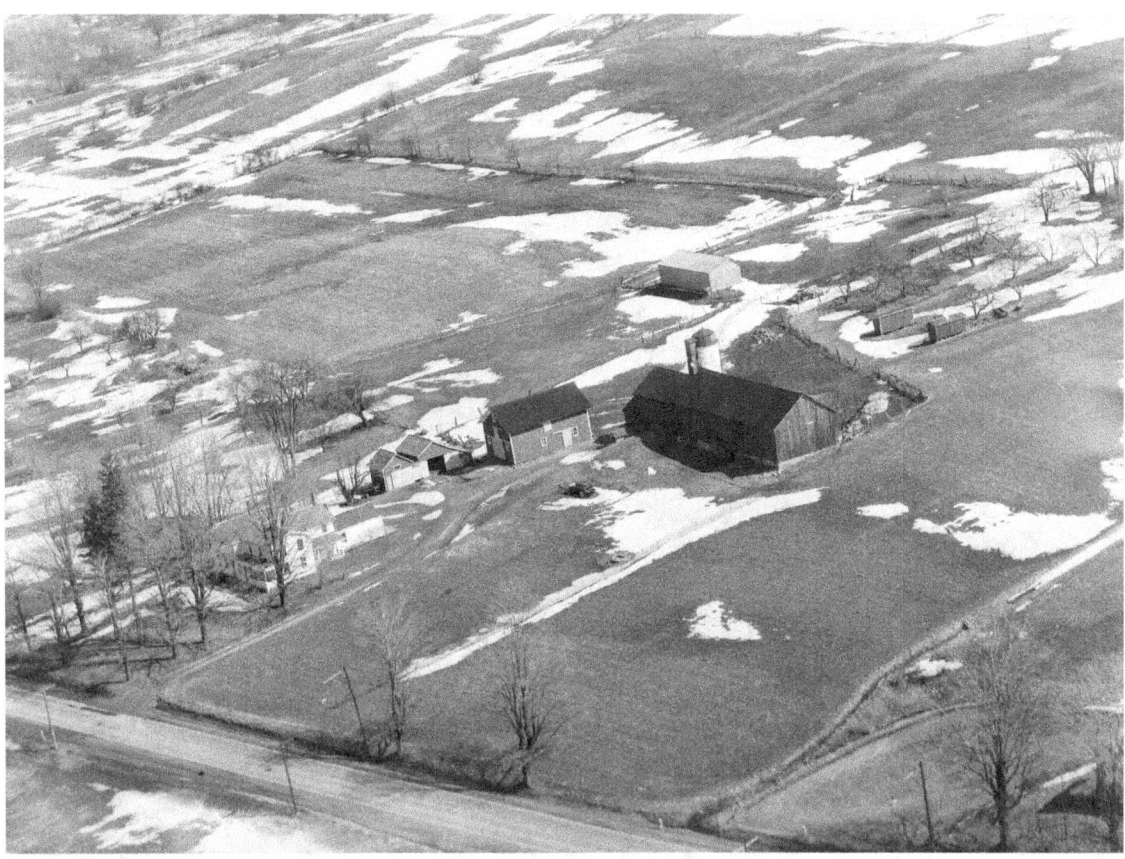

242-217 Richard Long farm, all barns torn down in 1999 except the horse barn built in 1883.

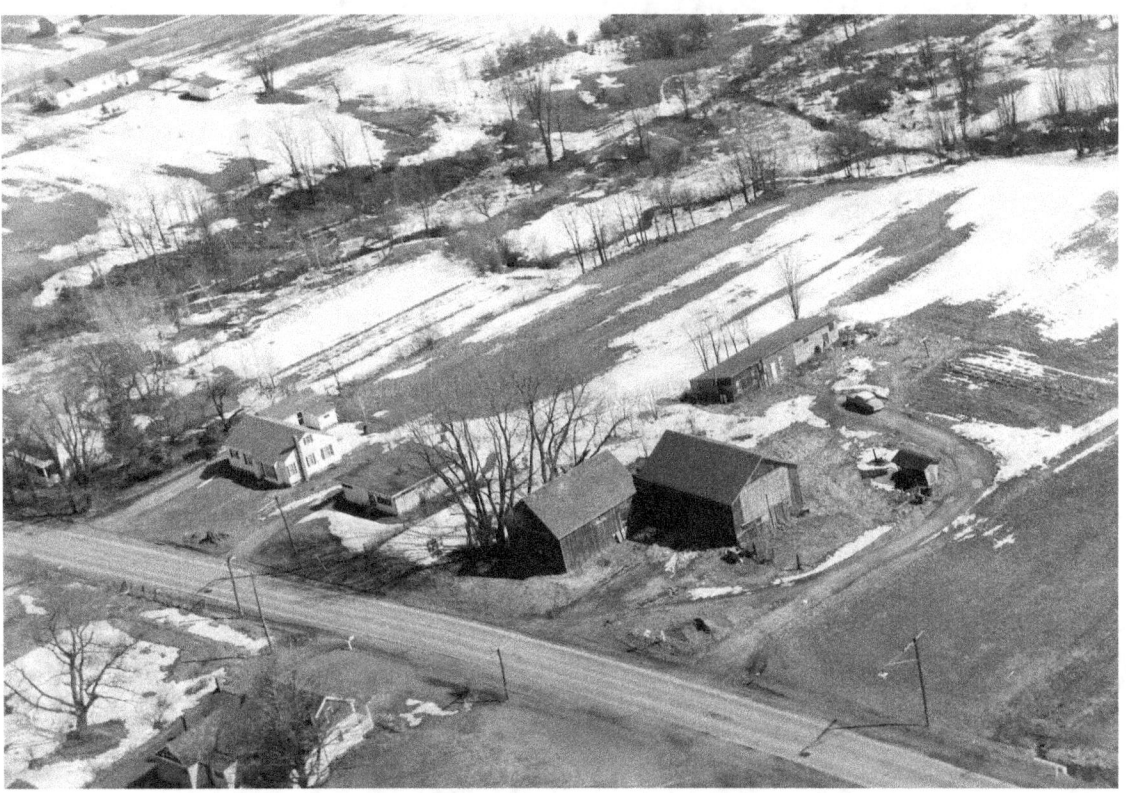

242-218 Robert Puttkammer farm, all barns gone.

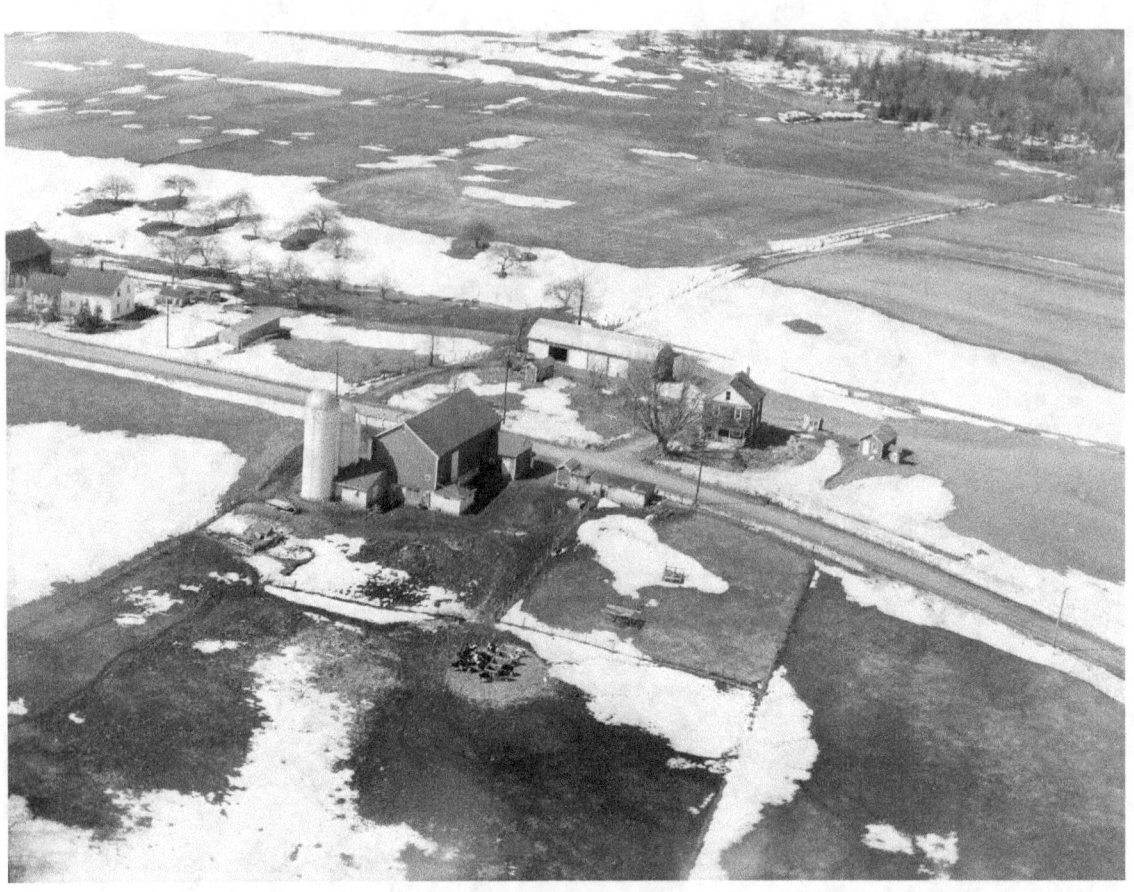

242-219 Naughton Brothers farm on Webb Road. All buildings still standing.

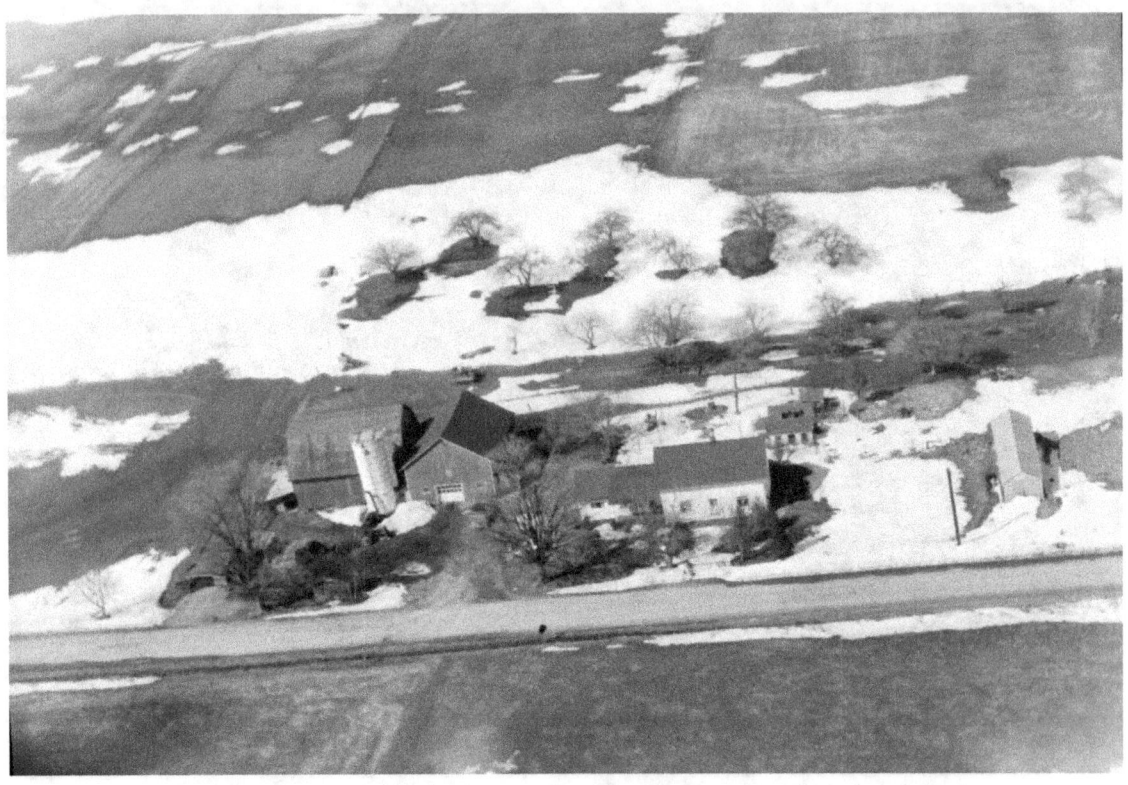

242-220 Rexford Parker farm on Webb Road. Barns burned in 1965.

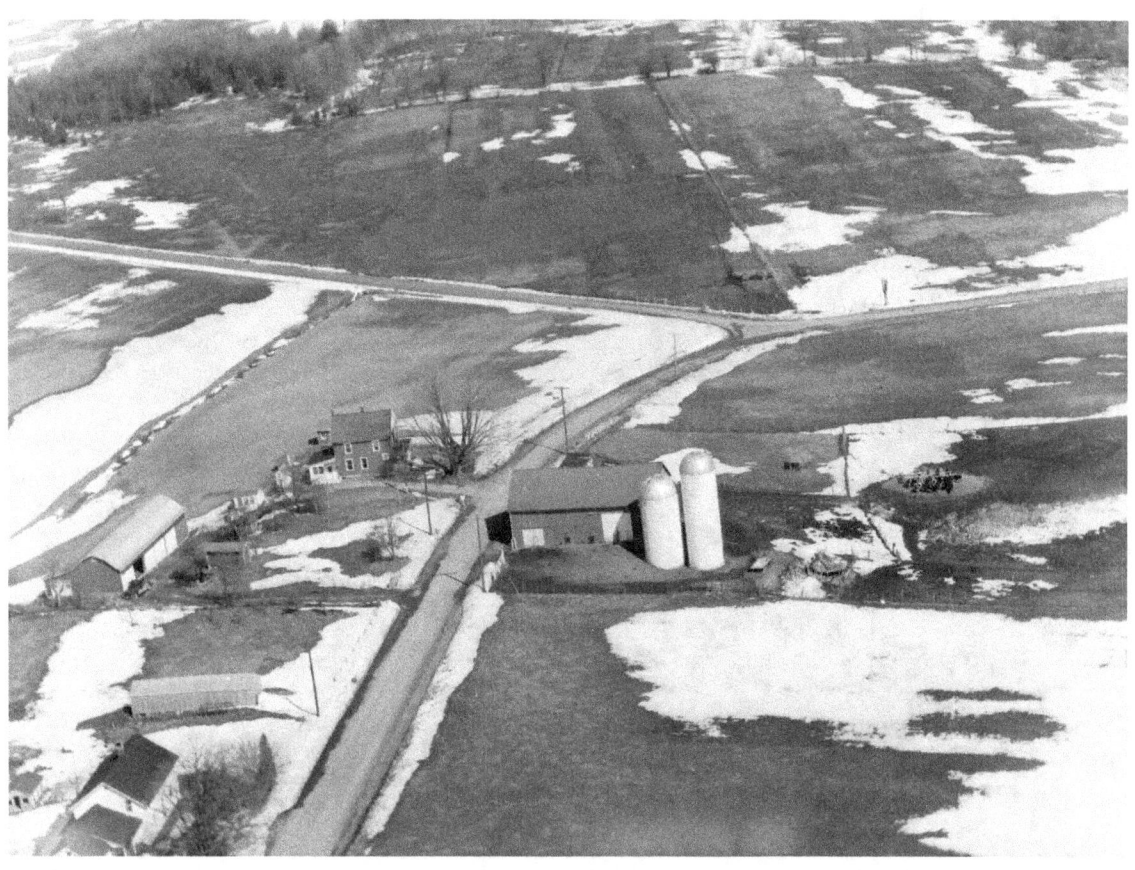

242-221 2nd view of Naughton Bros. farm on Webb Road.

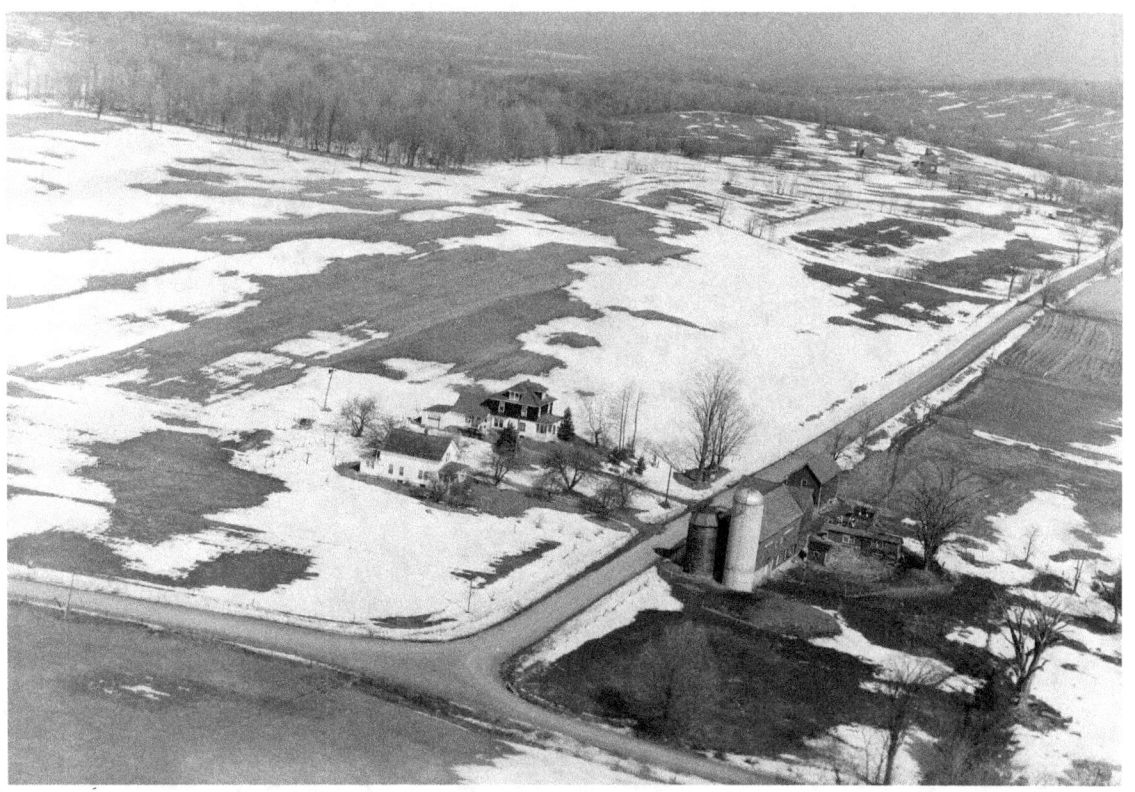

242-222 Earl McVoy farm on Webb Road. All buildings still standing.

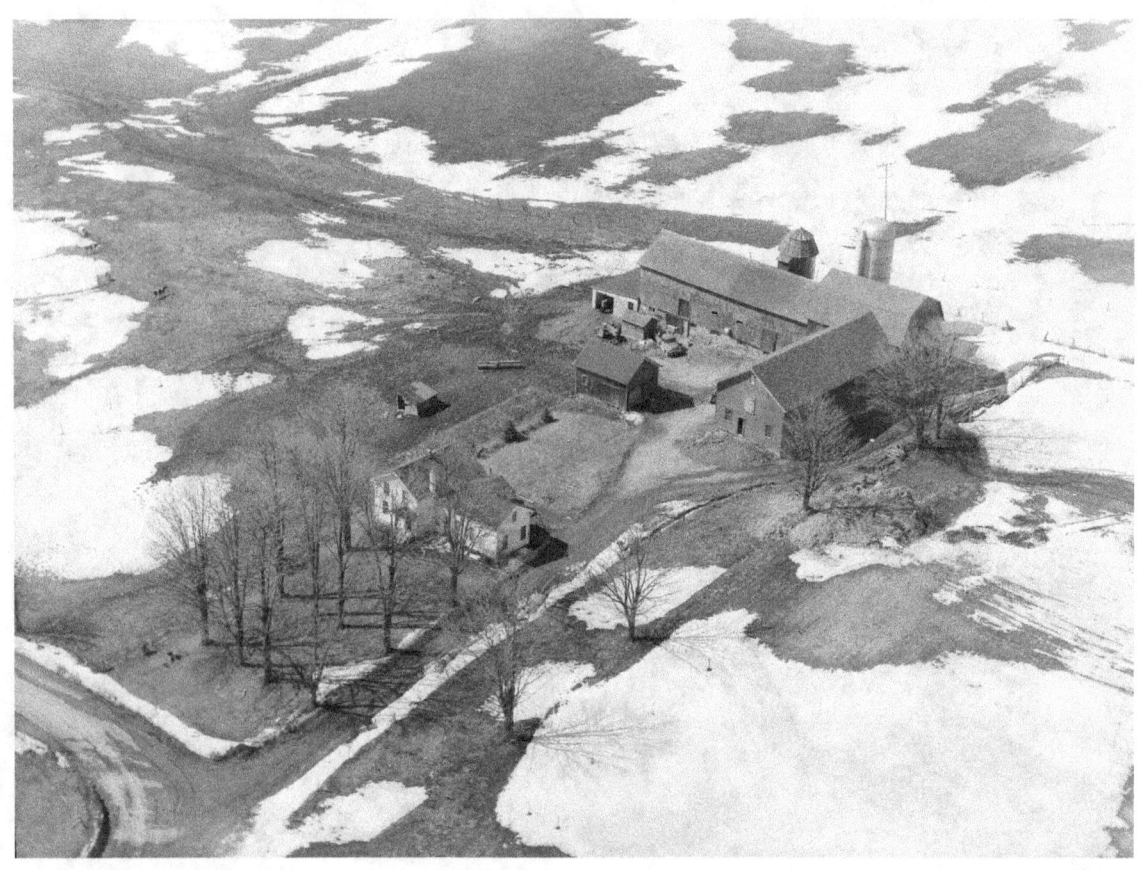

242-223 James McVoy farm on Webb Road, all buildings still standing.

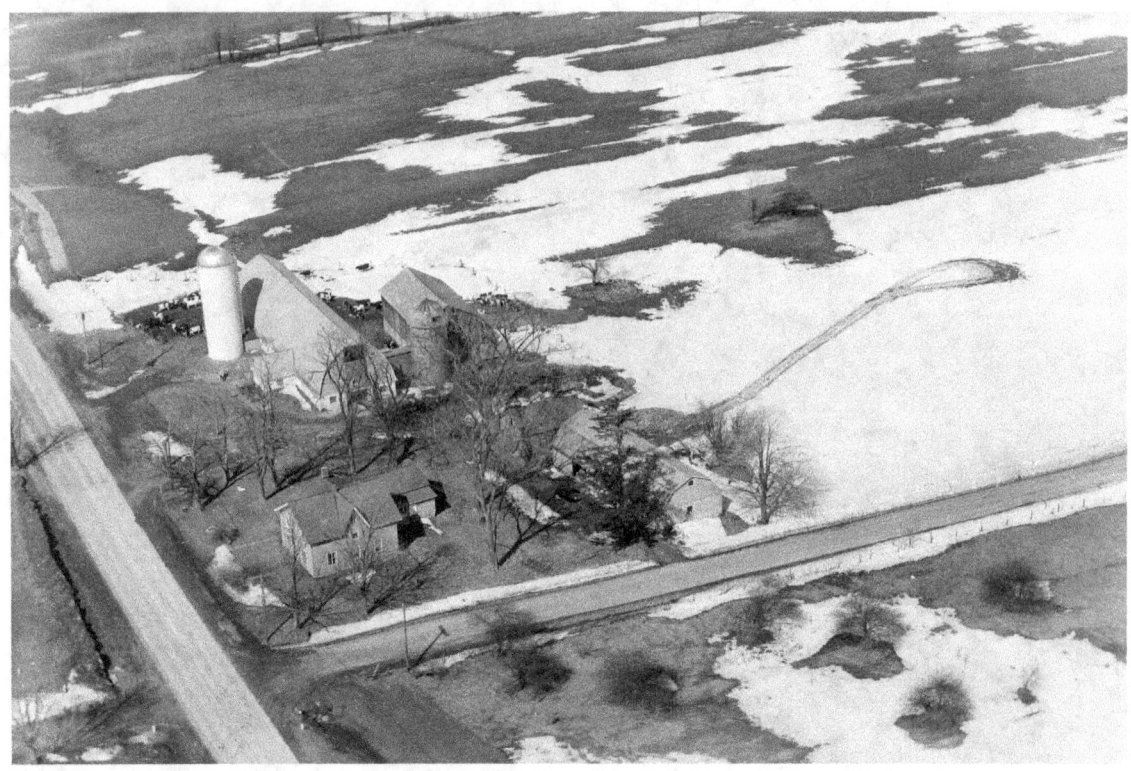

242-224 Bernard Aunger farm on Webb Road @ Route 20. Barn built in 1949 and still standing. Older barn in rear is no longer standing.

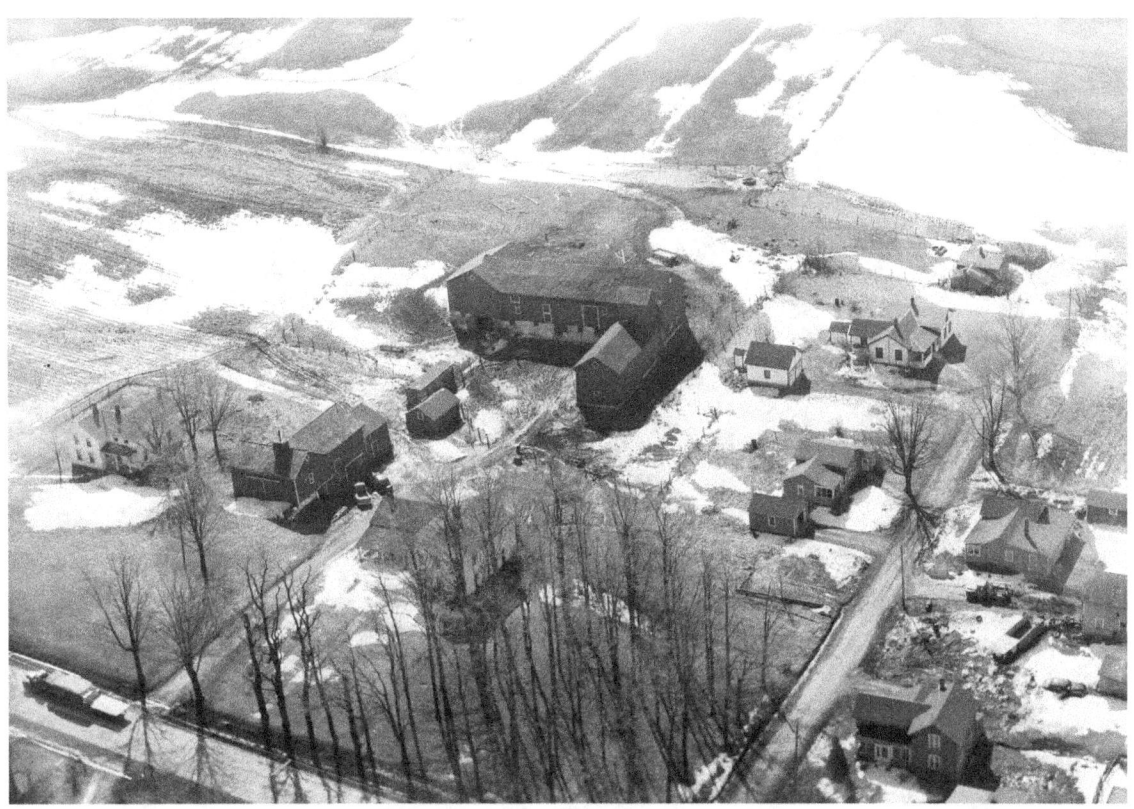

242-225 Thomas Ryder farm in LaFayette Village. "The Lane" on right. All barns gone now.

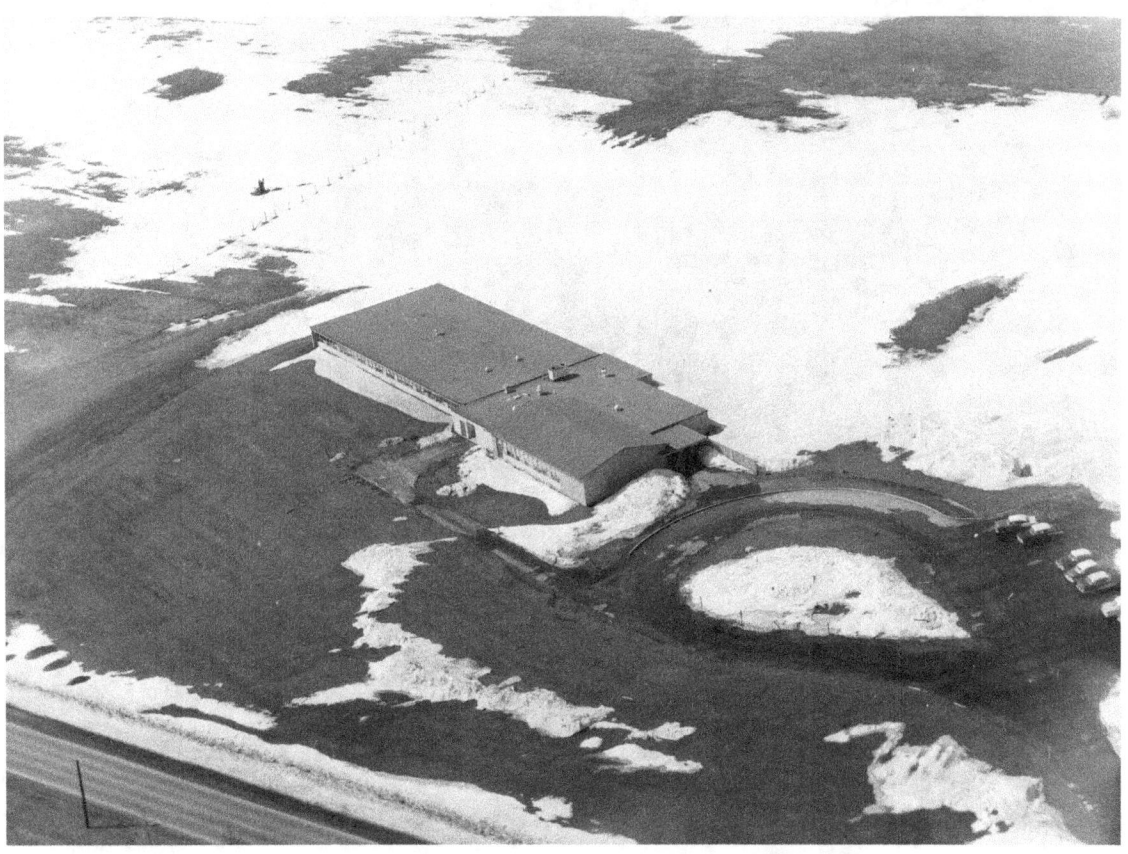

242-226 LaFayette Elementary School built in 1956. Closed in 1976, now apartments.

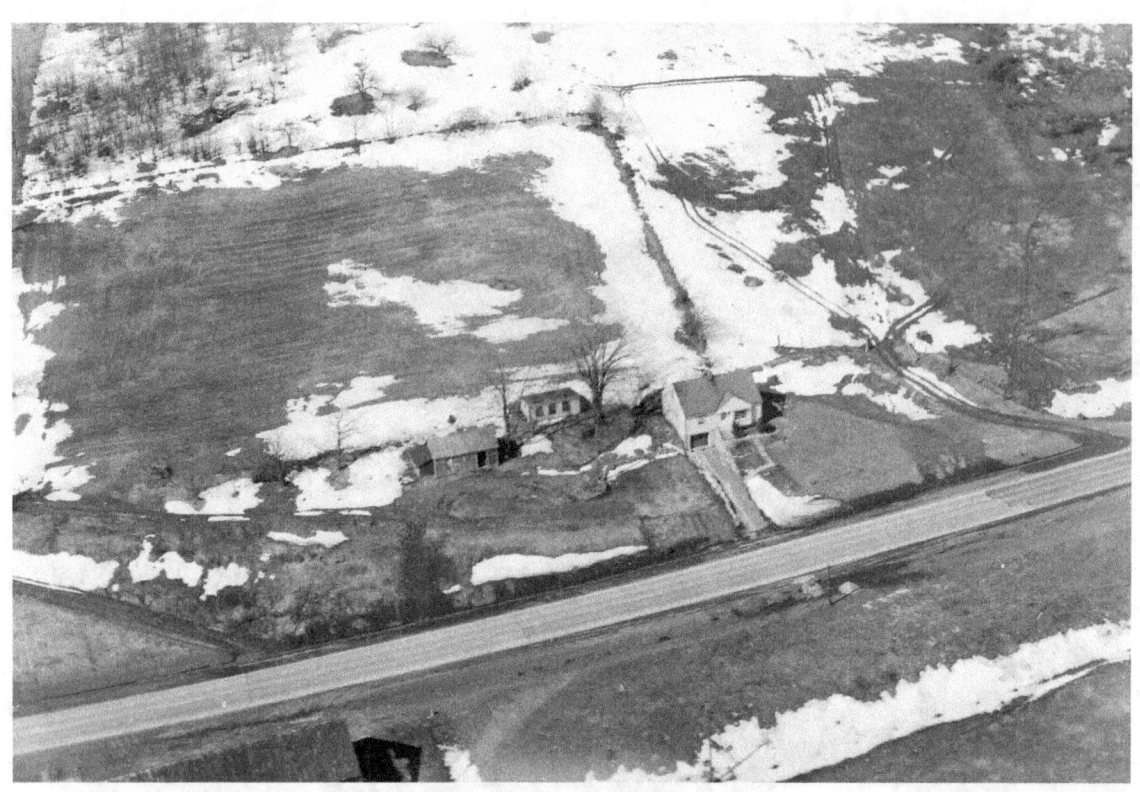

242-227 George Jochum house Route 20.

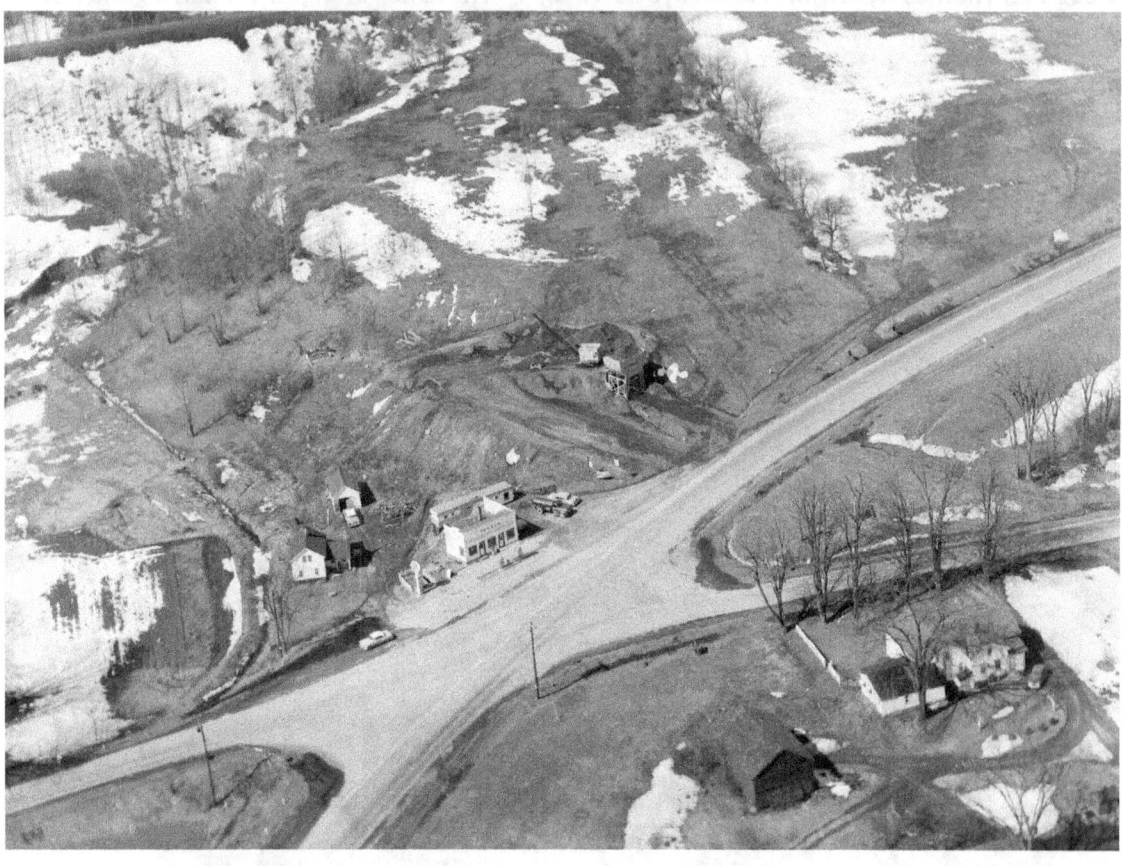

242-228 "Big Bend Gas Station" Route 20 @ Apulia Road.

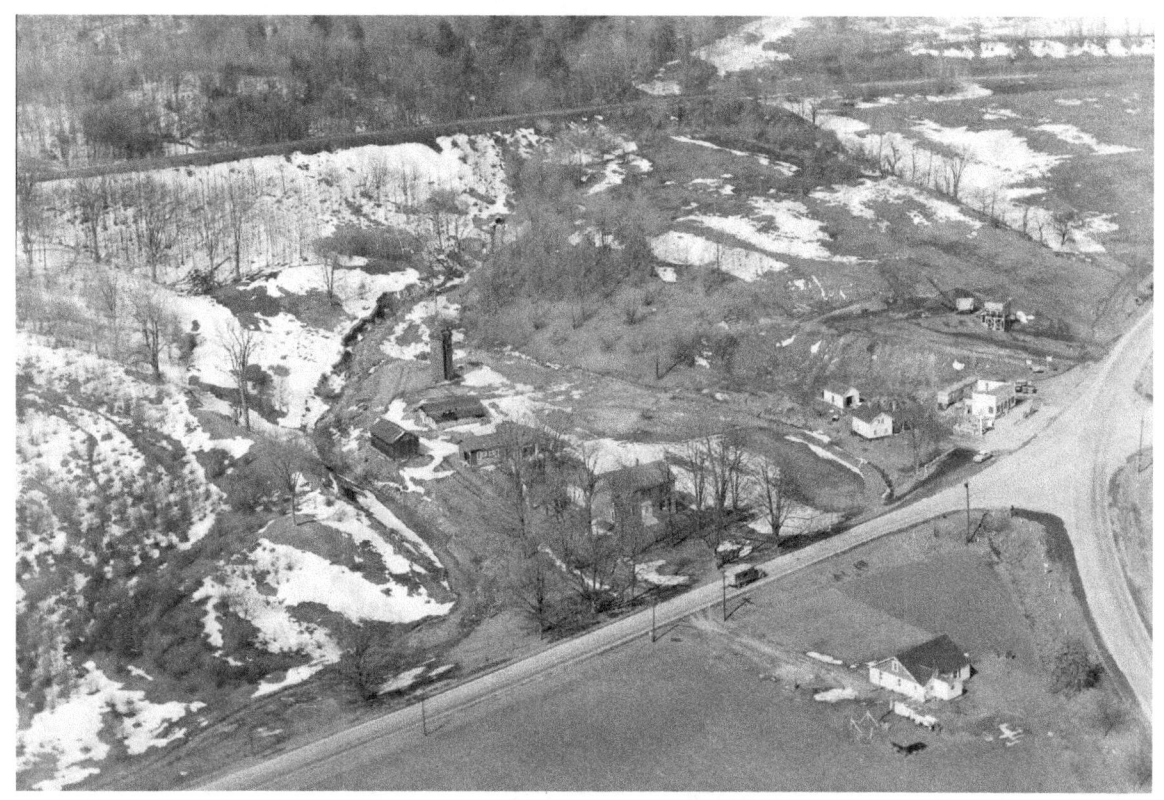

242-229 George Palmer brick house Apulia Road @ Route 20.

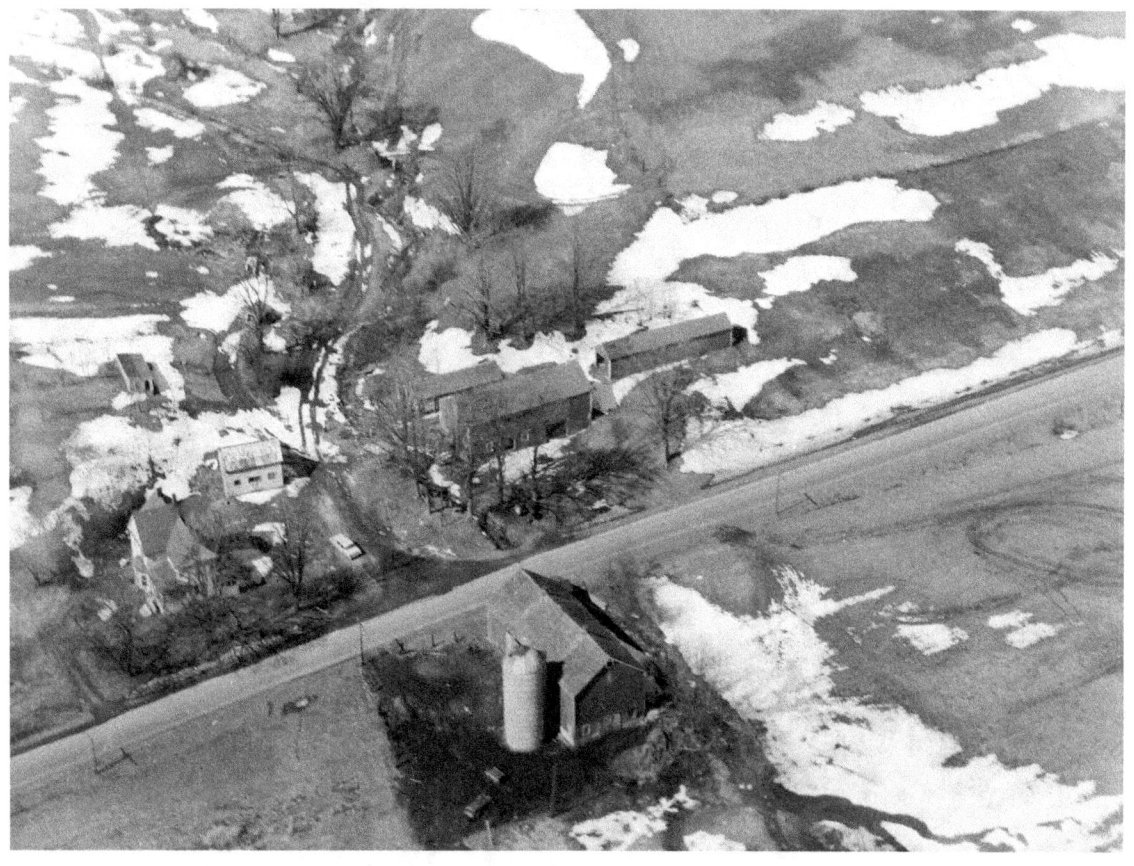

242-230 Ben Blum farm, Apulia Road. Buildings on west of road, upper side, are gone.

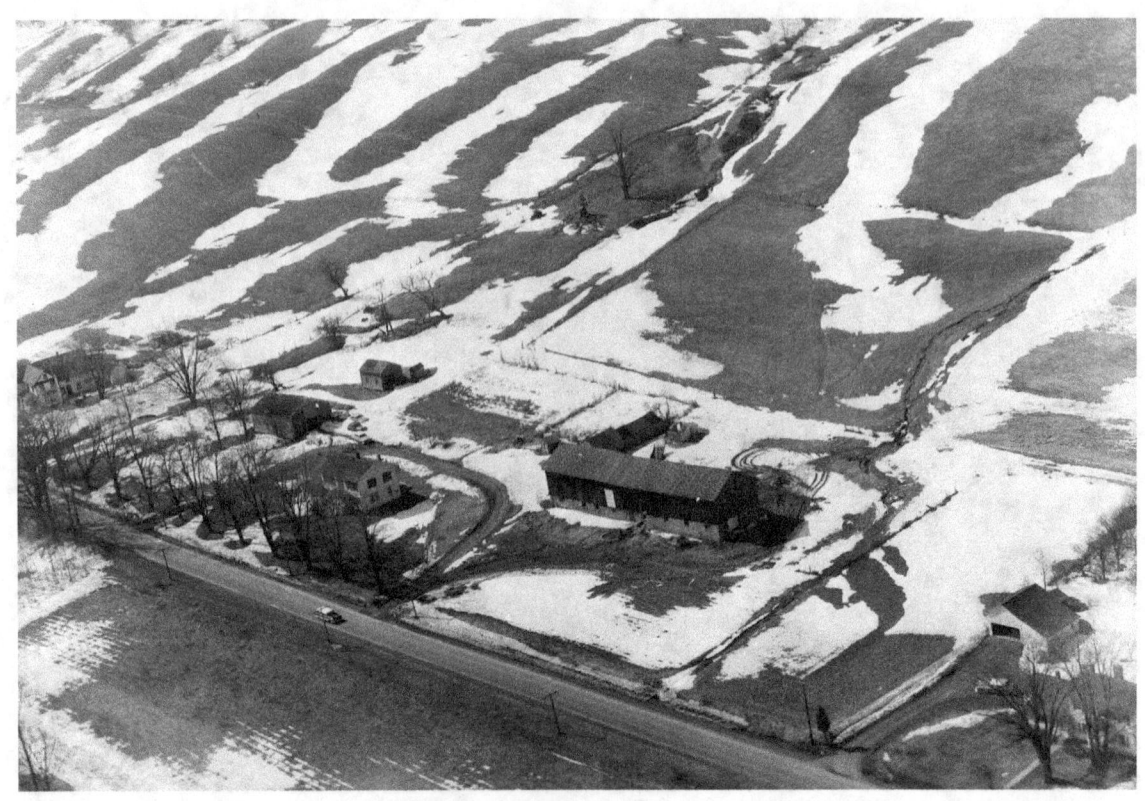

242-231 William Fox farm on Apulia Road. Barns fell down and farm sold to Joseph Bocak.

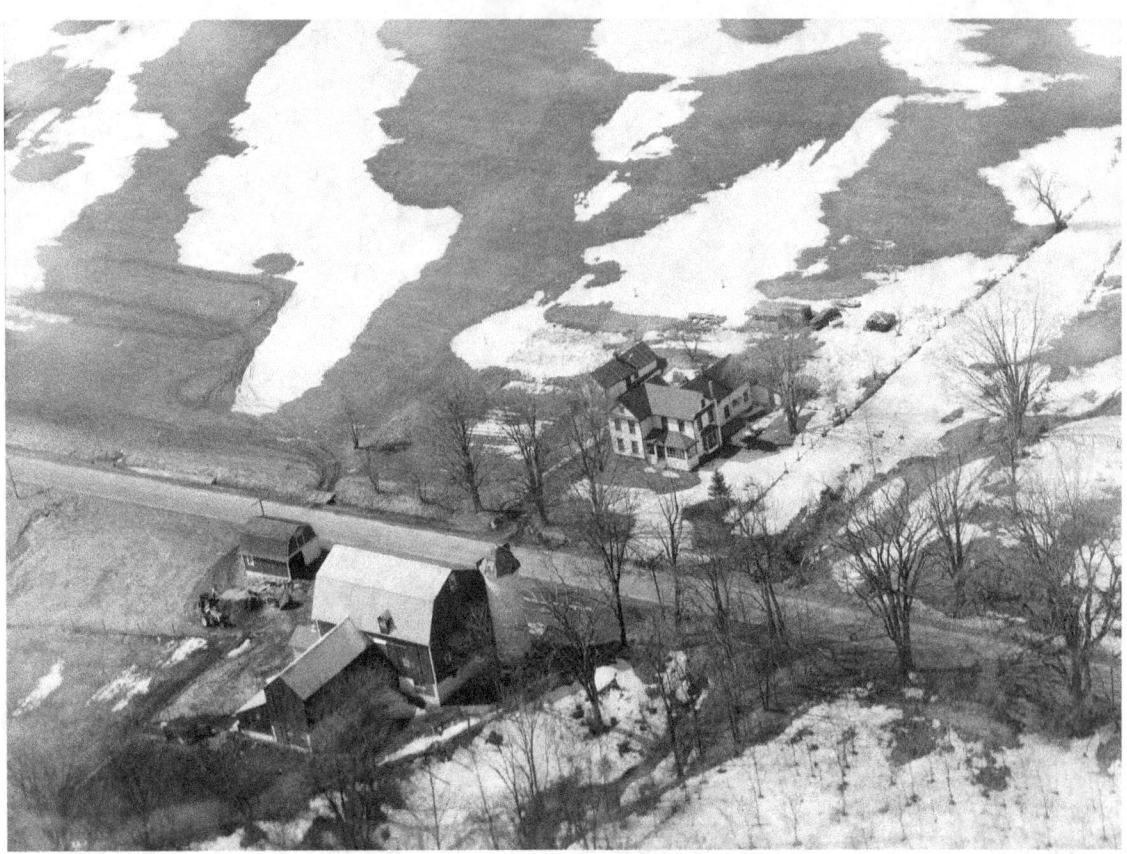

242-232 Joseph Bocak (formerly Leonard farm) Apulia Road. Main barn standing, house built in 1920.

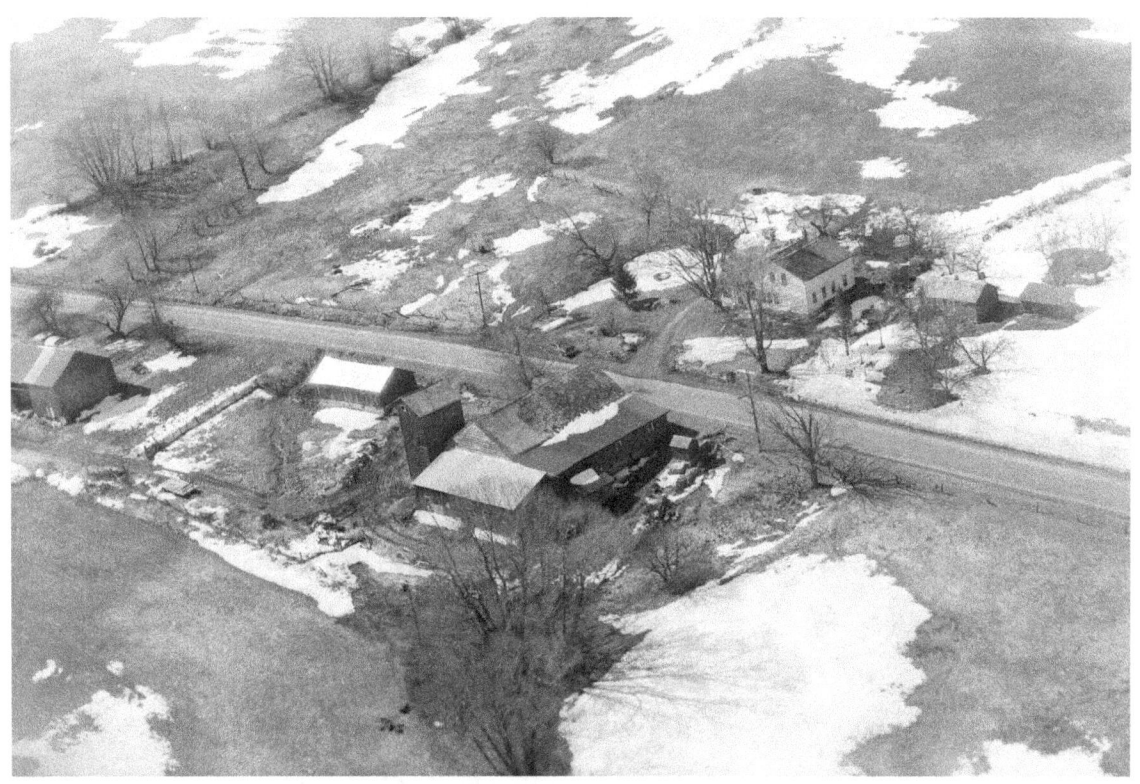

242-233 Clifford Vanderwalker farm Apulia Road. All buildings gone.

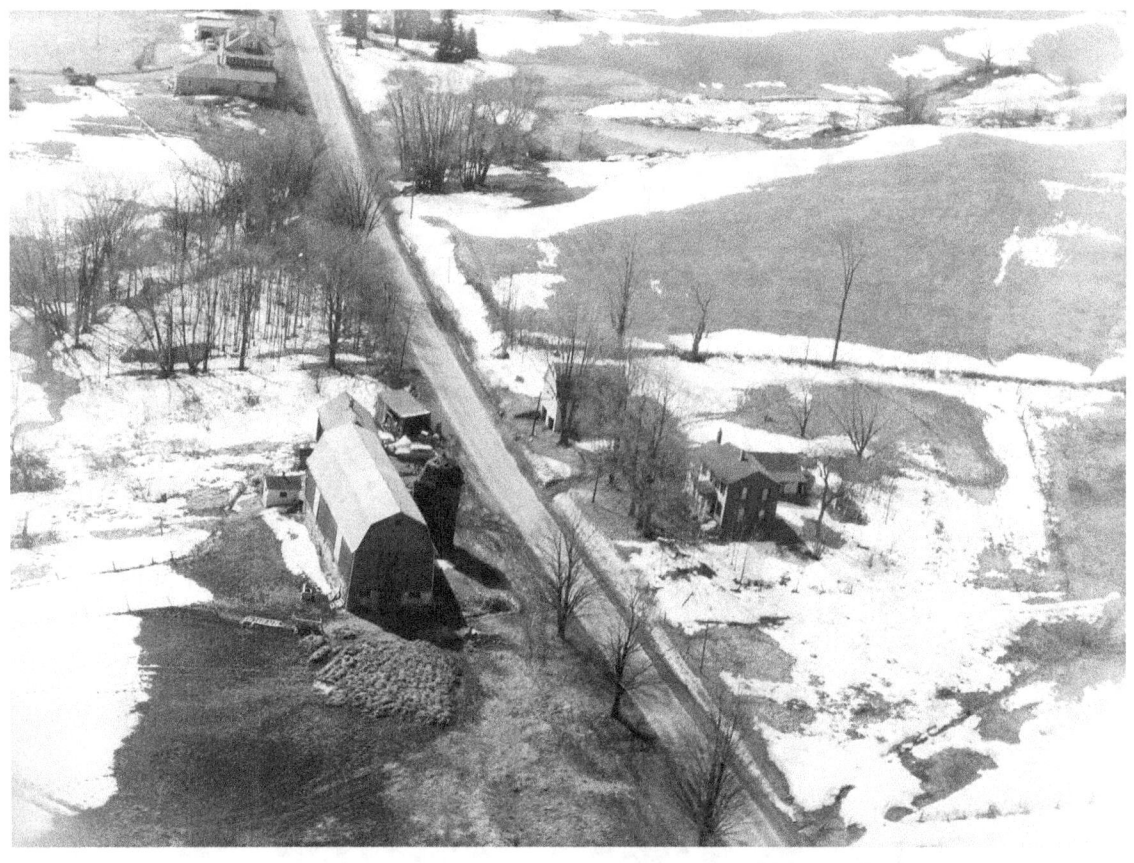

242-234 Ernest Sevier farm on Apulia Road. Barn built in 1916 and is still standing. Farm sold to Robert Park in 1959.

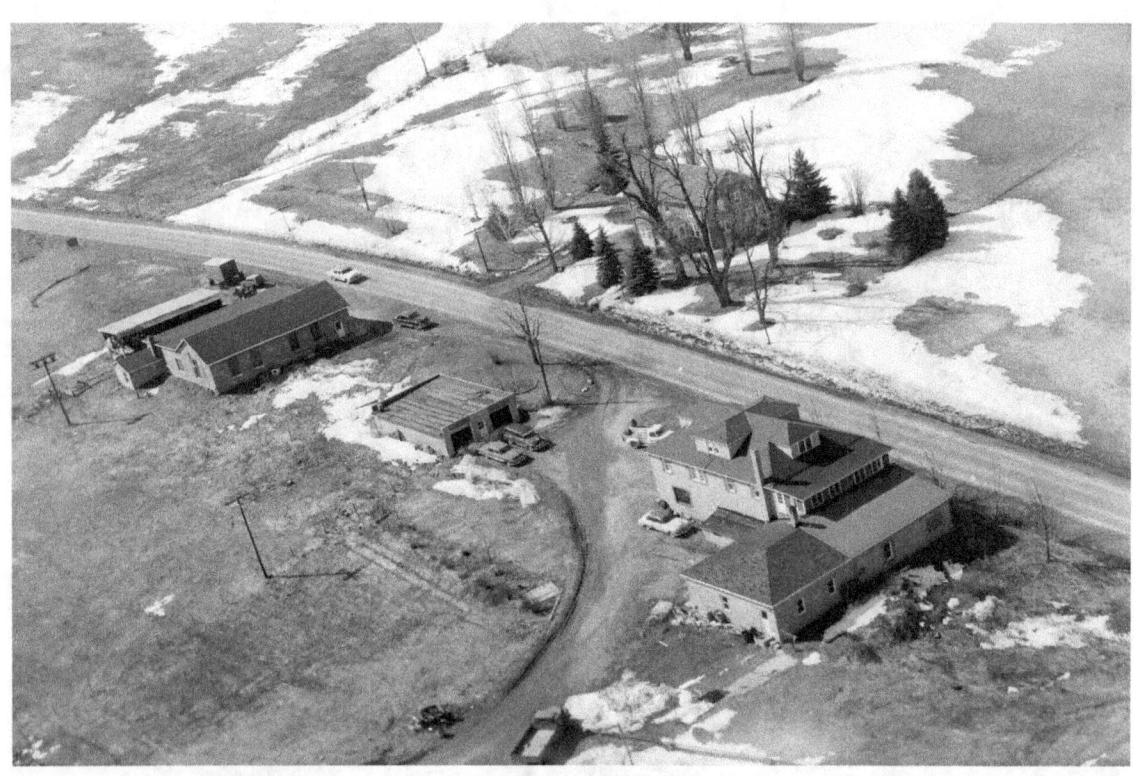

242-235 Hart's Rending Company on the right, Beebe & Butler on left. Town of Fabius starts on the left of photo.

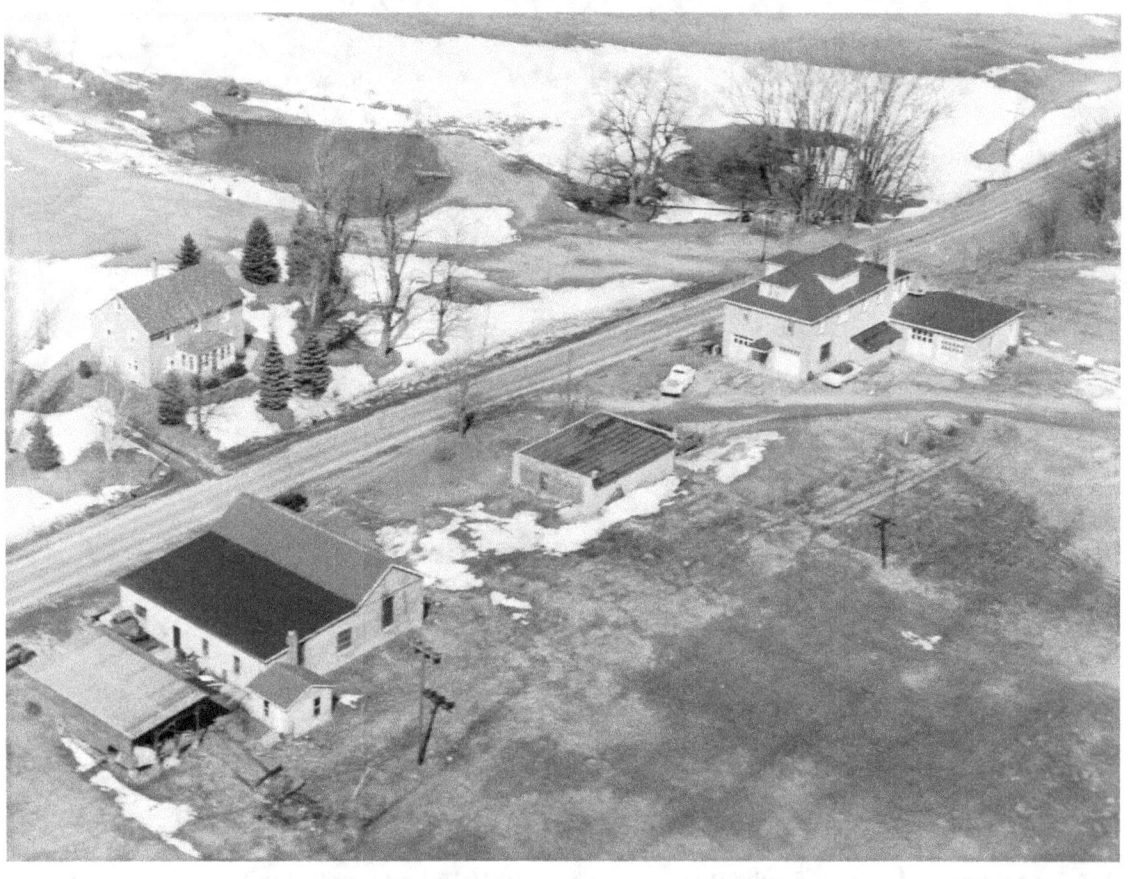

242-236 Beebe and Butler left, Hart's Rendering Company on right. Hart's now manufacture guns.

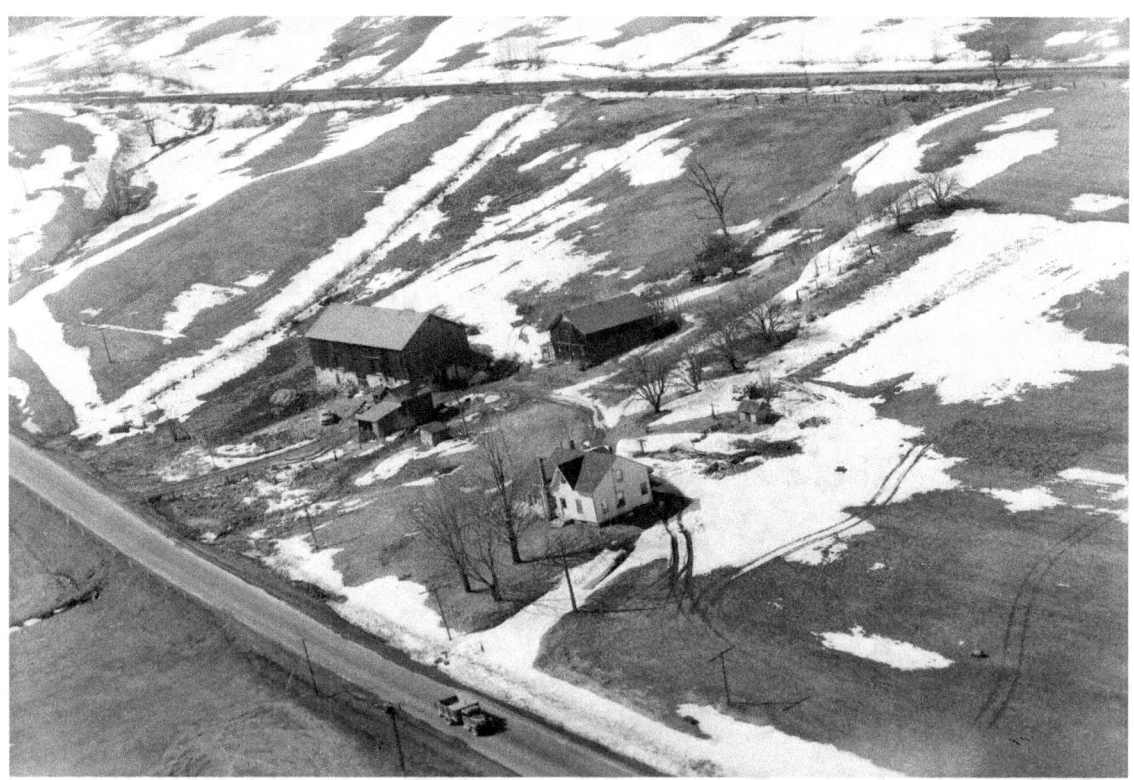

242-237 Vance Smith farm. Formerly the Jay and Howard Brown farm. All barns are gone now while house has been remodeled.

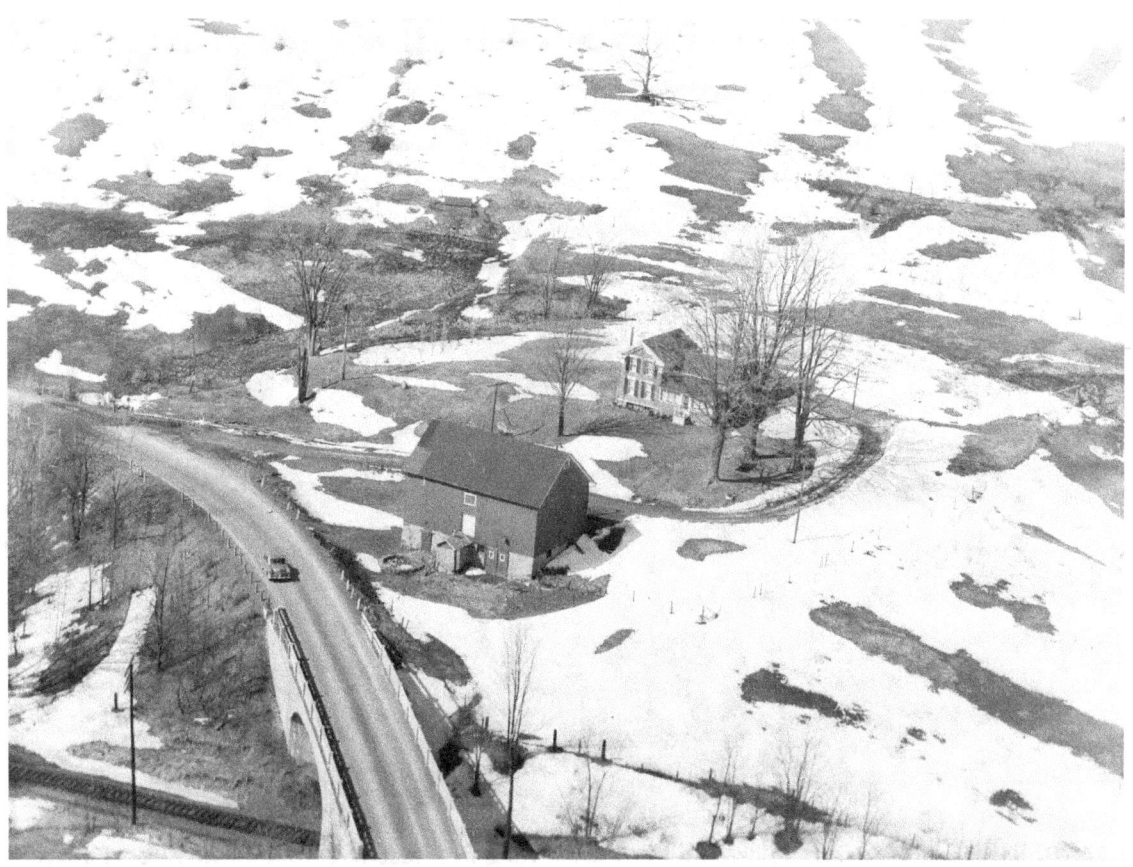

242-238 Fairchild formerly Jencks farm. Barn built in 1903, railroad bridge in 1916.

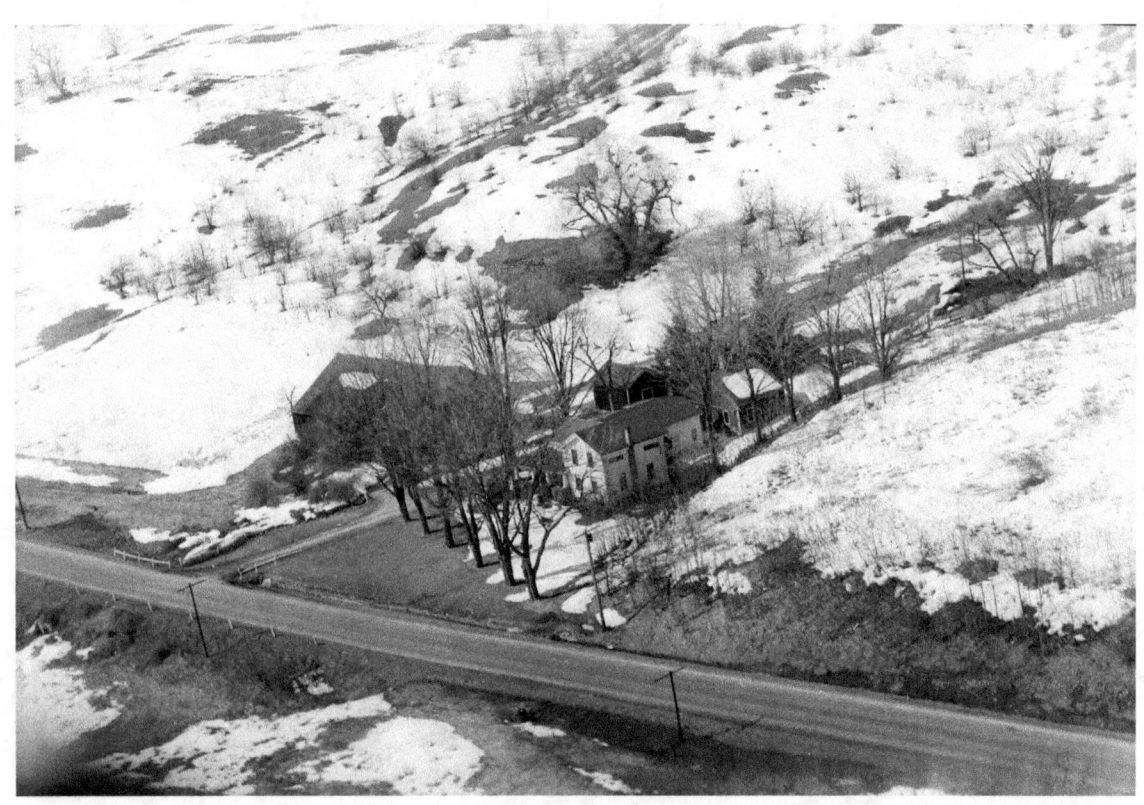

242-239 Edward and Teresa Tasker farm. Formerly the Irvin Mills place passed on to Teresa Tasker. Barn went down in 2010.

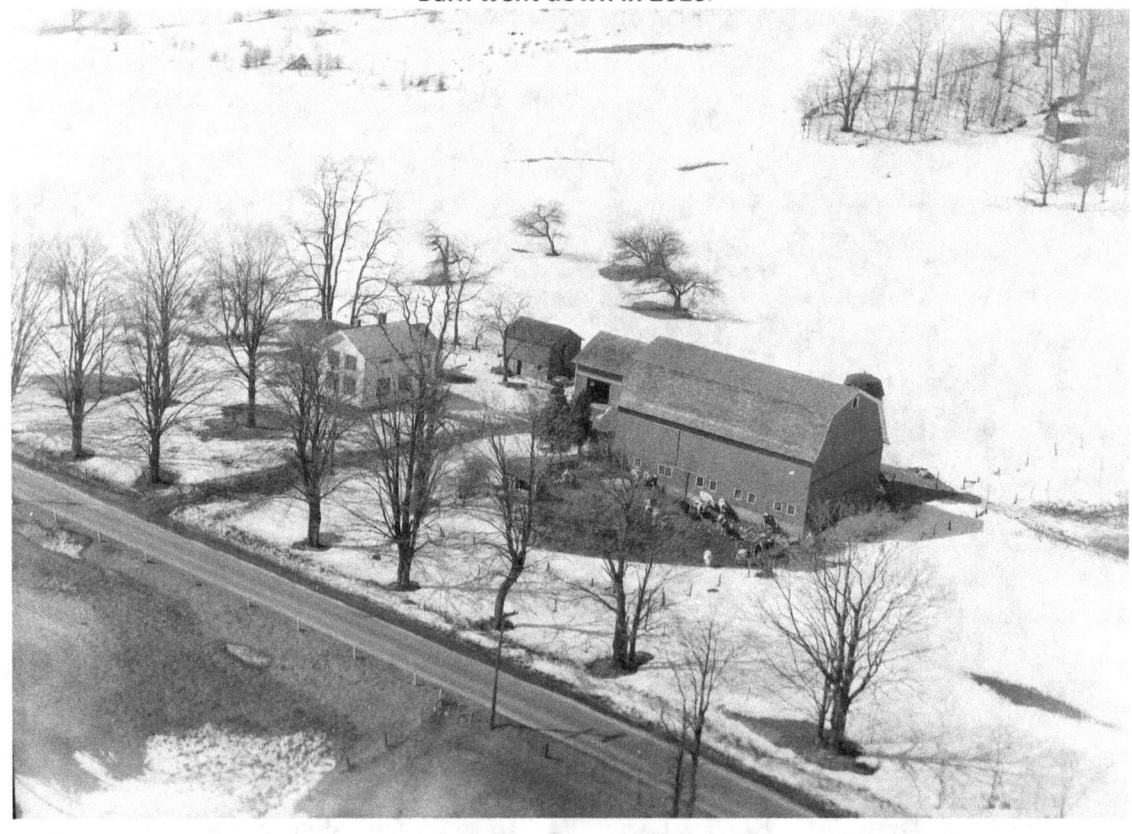

242-240 Robert Tompkins farm. Barn built in 1937 after a fire destroyed old barn. Robert braved the fire to save his cows and horses and was badly burned. He continued to farm for the next two decades.

www.ingramcontent.com/pod-product-compliance
Lightning Source LLC
Chambersburg PA
CBHW081148170526
45158CB00009BA/2770